Integrate
Crop Managem

033137

ROYAL AGRICULTURAL COLLEGE

D1385943

Sponsor:

ᴐh
Agrochemicals
Association

Supported by:

LANDBASE

LEAF

SAINSBURY'S

Integrated Crop Management

© 1996 The British Agrochemicals Association
4 Lincoln Court, Lincoln Road, Peterborough PE1 2RP

All rights reserved. No part of this publication may be reproduced, stored in a retrieval system, or transmitted, in any form or by any means, electronic, mechanical, photocopying, recording or otherwise, without prior permission of the copyright owners.

British Library Cataloguing in Publication Data.
A catalogue record for this publication is available from the British Library.

British Agrochemicals Association
Integrated Crop Management

ISBN 0 905598 05 9 /

Photographs courtesy of CWS Agriculture, The Game Conservancy Trust, John Deere Ltd and Profarma Ltd.

Designed by Major Design and Production, Nottingham and printed in Great Britain by Fisherprint Ltd, Peterborough PE1 5UL

Contents

1

Integrated Crop Management: The Way Forward

Most people have heard of Integrated Crop Management (ICM) but how many can say confidently they know what it means? More importantly, where do farmers and advisors find help and guidance on what is involved. Is ICM yet another catch phrase for a method of farming that is best left to others? In truth, ICM is something that affects everyone – not only farmers but also consumers – and it presents a realistic solution to many of the problems facing agriculture.

In the Western World we are fortunate to have a plentiful supply of wholesome, high quality food at affordable prices. Spectacular improvements in agricultural efficiency and productivity over the past 50 years have made this possible. Faced with the challenge of an increasing demand for food and a steady loss of productive land to industrial and urban growth, farming methods have become more sophisticated. By the skilful adoption of new technologies in machinery, plant breeding, fertilisers and pesticides, farmers have matched supply to demand.

...the price of progress

Some would argue that there has been a price to pay for this success. People see surplus production as wasteful of natural resources and money, but few would opt for the alternative – shortage – which is so evident in other parts of the world.

Nevertheless it cannot be denied that mistakes have been made and the march of agricultural progress has left its scars. Hedgerows and other wildlife habitats have been removed to accommodate the use of bigger, more powerful machinery which, in turn, has sometimes damaged soil structure and drainage. The original Common Agricultural Policy encouraged the trend towards monoculture with the result that over-use of fertilisers and pesticides has contributed to a reduction in biodiversity. Enhanced levels of nitrates and some pesticides are turning up in drinking water, albeit at levels far below those likely to cause any damage to health.

...caring for the environment

The result of all this is that, with a full belly of food taken for granted, the public's message to farmers is that they must take more care about the environment of which they are the custodians. There is nothing reprehensible about this: indeed it is to be welcomed as part of an overall drive against the depletion of finite natural resources.

Sir John Harvey Jones is right when he says that "the pursuit of better, more environmentally friendly, methods of production will bring business rewards in their own right". Although his words refer to all businesses, they could not be more true for farming. In practice, agriculture has been addressing these issues for years and industries like machinery, plant breeding and pesticides can all point to significant technological advances. The problem is that farming is not well understood by the general public and it is certainly not appreciated as being the provider of produce on the supermarket shelf.

...meeting the challenge

The challenge to agriculture is to find a means of getting the message across. Adverse public opinion is a powerful influence on politicians. In response to this pressure, countries like Sweden, Denmark and Holland have imposed mandatory reduction targets of 50% in the use of pesticides. Denmark and Belgium have introduced taxes to reduce pesticide use. At Community level there is already a Directive in place (the Nitrate Directive) that requires Member States to limit nitrates coming from manures and inorganic sources. In UK this has resulted in the designation of Nitrate Vulnerable Zones.

If British farming is to avoid the imposition of draconian and impractical restraints that may win votes but ignore sound science, then it needs to meet its critics by showing that environmental responsibility can sit hand in hand with profit and productivity achieved by the judicious use of inputs. This is Integrated Crop Management.

...definitions and meanings

What the words mean

- *Integrated*: a site specific management system for the whole farm;
- *Crop*: involvement of all aspects of crop husbandry – not just crop protection;
- *Management*: planning, setting targets and monitoring achievement.

There are plenty of definitions of ICM (see end of this chapter), but common to all of them are phrases like 'environmental responsibility', 'social acceptability' and 'ecological sensitivity'. But there is more to it than this. ICM is a system that balances these features with running an economically viable business. Food production must go on, and that requires a healthy and profitable agricultural industry.

Integrated is a key word because ICM is a combination of farming practices, including the use of rotations, appropriate cultivations, choice of variety and the judicious use of fertilisers and pesticides, with measures to preserve and protect the environment. It involves everything that happens on the farm, but it starts with the farm itself and therefore it is site specific. Whatever else may be changed, the features of the farm in terms of its topography, buildings and climate cannot be altered. Some of these factors will influence what can be achieved so a thorough survey of the site is an essential starting point.

Crop appears in the title because ICM involves all aspects of crop husbandry, such as variety selection, cultivation, drilling date, harvest and storage methods and marketing. It is not just crop protection, which is often referred to as integrated pest management (IPM). IPM is just the crop protection part of ICM.

Above all, ICM is a systematised approach to farming that requires *management* in the form of planning, setting targets and monitoring achievement.

...critical self-examination

We all get into bad habits with habitual tasks such as driving a car. Some people recognise this and go back for some lessons or take an advanced driving test. For most people, however, the bad habits can become the norm and, unless they lead to trouble, they are seldom questioned. Farming is no exception.

The first stage of implementation of an ICM system is to step back and take a hard critical look at existing practices. The LEAF environmental audit is an excellent and painless way of doing this because it is arranged as a series of self-assessment forms. Not only can it help to identify the bad habits but, if carried out annually, it provides a means of monitoring progress.

LEAF (Linking Environment and Farming)

- A charitable organisation committed to the concept of a viable agriculture that is environmentally and socially acceptable;

- Funded by over 60 industry bodies and companies together with farmer members;

- Promotes the responsible and economic use of the best of traditional and modern farming methods;

- The LEAF environmental audit helps farmers to carry out a self assessment of current practice and identify a farm environment management strategy;

- LEAF provides advice and guidance by example through a network of LEAF farms in UK;

- A member of the Integrated Arable Crop Production Alliance (IACPA) which co-ordinates the efforts of the seven leading UK organisations involved in Integrated Crop Management.

LEAF is based at the National Agricultural Centre, Stoneleigh, Coventry, Warwickshire (Telephone: 01203 413911).

Advanced driving is concerned with a thorough knowledge of the rules and regulations, awareness of the impact of your actions on others and looking and planning ahead for possible hazards. ICM requires the same qualities – it is the advanced driving test of farming. It is not a set of hard and fast rules but a set of guidelines to follow in the particular and unique circumstances of any particular farm. It not only addresses the fundamentals of best practice, but it is also concerned with attention to detail. This includes, for example, crop rotations, soil and cultivation practices, crop nutrition strategy, crop protection, wildlife and landscape management, energy conservation, pollution control and waste disposal planning.

...accountability and transparency

Change is necessary in order to gain public and political confidence in the way our food is produced. In order to allay public concerns, farmers and growers must not only act responsibly, but must be seen to do so. Transparency and accountability are the building bricks on which public confidence can be built. Considerable strides towards this have been made in a joint initiative between the National Farmers Union, the major retailers, including Sainsbury's and food processors to set protocols of practice which growers have to adopt, notably in the way they manage their pesticide programmes in most fruit and vegetable crops.

Adoption of the principles of ICM adds professionalism to an already skilled industry. It enables its practitioners to show how modern farming practices can produce quality food and ensure a thriving and healthy environment.

But ICM is not a recipe for wholesale change. Most farmers are already well down the road towards adoption of ICM principles and it is now a case of fine tuning. What it requires is the courage and flexibility to look at everything that happens on the farm – some of it the habits of a lifetime – and ask the question: 'Could it be done better?'

In a nutshell, ICM is skills-intensive, rather than input-intensive farming. This does not suggest that inputs must necessarily be reduced, but they should certainly be optimised to achieve maximum benefit with minimum impact. As with any system, it is essential that it is achievable and measurable. Detailed practical advice is a key element. In recognition of this, the British Agrochemicals Association has sponsored a complete resources pack on ICM for anyone involved in training. It was made with strong financial and technical support from ATB-Landbase, LEAF and Sainsbury's. It examines all the main areas of farming practice in nine detailed modules.

...providing a better understanding

In this booklet the key points are discussed and elaborated. The intention is to provide a guide for those who wish to have a better understanding of arable farming and to gain a grasp of the scope of ICM, what it involves and some of the problems its practitioners have to face.

Integrated Crop Management – some definitions

- The efficient profitable production of crops in harmony with nature for our benefit and that of future generations.

- An holistic pattern of land use which integrates natural resources and regulation mechanisms into farming practices to achieve a maximum but stepwise replacement of off-farm inputs to secure high quality food and to sustain income.

- A whole farm policy, combining rotations with targeted use of pesticides and fertilisers, cultivation choice, variety selection together with a positive management plan of landscape and wildlife features.

- A comprehensive system of modern husbandry practice.

- Balancing economic production with environmental responsibility.

- The choice of a balanced crop rotation which can reduce pest, disease and weed problems whilst maintaining soil structure and fertility.

- A cropping strategy in which the farmer seeks to conserve and enhance the environment while economically producing safe, wholesome food. Its long term aim is to optimise the needs of consumers, society, the environment and the farmer.

- A combination of responsible farming practices which balance the economic production of crops with measures which conserve and enhance the environment.

- The concept of a viable agriculture which is environmentally and socially acceptable and ensures the continuity of supply of wholesome, affordable food while conserving and enhancing the fabric and wildlife of the British countryside for future generations.

- A proven crop rotation backed up by judicious management whose aim is to keep inputs to a minimum while maintaining profitability at conventional farming levels.

- A concept which blends the best of traditional farming methods with the environmentally sensitive use of modern technology.

- A management system which employs controlled inputs to achieve sustained profitability with minimum environmental impact, but with sufficient flexibility to meet natural and market challenges economically.

2

The Site

Making the best of what you have

The farm site is a combination of its physical features, climate and location. Little can be done to change these properties, but it is important in any management system to assess the extent to which the things that cannot be altered may constrain those that can. The term *integrated* in ICM means that it is a combination of responsible farming practices in a whole farm policy. ICM cannot be practised on any one field, or on any one crop, or in any one year. The geographical location of the farm is fixed, and the physical features cannot be altered significantly. Yet it is clear that both these factors may be an important influence in governing what may, or may not, be achievable in an ICM system. Location and climate may rule out certain crops, while topography and soil type can also dictate cultivation methods and influence energy consumption. This is why ICM does not seek to lay down a set of hard and fast rules but instead gives guidance on what has to considered and what questions need to be asked about current practices.

A survey of the physical nature of the farm itself, together with other features, such as locality and climate, is the starting point. A motorist uses a road map when planning an unfamiliar route. Similarly, a golfer playing a strange course will find hidden dangers and pitfalls unless he carries a course plan. A farm site survey fulfils much the same objective: its purpose is to identify those features that may be an asset in ICM as well as those that will be limiting factors.

Mapping the physical features

An accurate farm map is essential. This should be sufficiently detailed to show not only the farm layout with field sizes but also the nature of all field boundaries and water courses, locations of all buildings, overhead power and telephone lines. In addition, all public rights of way and any fixed natural features such as archaeological sites and rocky outcrops need to be noted. These are the fixed features and detailed information such as the height of power lines or the nature of water courses is necessary for ICM planning. The slopes and aspects of the fields will also have a significant bearing on crop choice and cultivation.

Soil is the key to successful Integrated Crop Management. Knowledge of its physical characteristics needs to be supplemented with information about its structure and drainage together with those properties that can be altered, such as acidity and compaction. The state of repair of all fences, hedges and walls needs to be checked to ensure that they adequately fulfil their intended function, for example as windbreaks or livestock proofing.

Water may be free flowing or stagnant, weed infested, polluted, used for irrigation or drainage. A river may have fishing rights and there may be public right of access, both of which might affect farm management decisions. Whatever the circumstances, water is certain to be an important wildlife haven and it is also the part of the farm environment most likely to be at risk from pollution. The farm map should show as much detail as possible.

Finally the map should show detail of the age, species composition and use of woodland and hedgerows as well as the location of other wildlife habitats.

Practical implications

Climate has an important influence on the type of crops that be grown satisfactorily. Altitude can affect climate in a number of ways. The mean temperature drops about 0.5°C for every 90m rise above sea level and every 15m rise shortens the growing season by about two days. Light interception is governed by aspect and a north-facing slope may be, on average, 1°C cooler than a slope facing south. In addition, field slopes in combination with other features such as hollows, banks, walls and hedges can create frost pockets which must be avoided where sensitive early crops such as potatoes are to be grown.

Field topography is therefore one important factor in determining the farm cropping plan. Some crops need a favourable south facing aspect; others may require shelter from wind or good drainage. Slopes and soil type will also determine the machinery that can operate and the potential for wind or water erosion.

Some fields may be identified as areas vulnerable to pollution, such as fertiliser or pesticide run-off, and this, too, will have a bearing on cropping. Field gateways must obviously be wide enough to allow machinery access and overhead telegraph and power lines must not impede its use. Maintenance costs must be accounted for in the farm plan.

...woodland, water and wildlife

As well as being fixed physical features of the farm, woodland and water are valuable components of the overall farm strategy. Woodland, for example, may have commercial value as forestry, it may be a source of farm building material, it may provide fuel or act as a useful windbreak. There may be public footpaths through it and it is certain to be a haven for a rich diversity of wildlife.

Similarly, water may be a source of irrigation water while at the same time providing landscape and amenity value. Efficient water conservation is a topic of increasing importance. In today's market, farmers and growers have to ensure that they can meet a continuing demand from consumers and retailers of produce. To achieve this they may often need the option of irrigating during the summer. Constructing reservoirs to store water during the wet months of the year requires capital outlay and careful planning. Guidance is available from MAFF on managing farm water resources in order to meet market requirements or avoid losses in drought years.

Advice on efficient water conservation

MAFF leaflets giving practical guidance are:

- *Winter Storage Reservoirs* –a detailed step by step guide to planning, constructing and operating a reservoir;

- *Best Irrigation Practice* –advice on how to cope with irrigation restrictions during the growing season;

- *Irrigation Scheduling* –guidance on how to apply the right amount of water at the right time.

...buildings

Neighbouring domestic premises are particularly important because their occupants will not only be able to see much of the activity on the farm, but they will also be in the front line if anything goes wrong. This might range from spray drift damage to gardens, to pollution by noise or smells from the farm. Unoccupied buildings might well be a haven for bats and owls but they may also house rats and mice. Furthermore they may be Listed buildings which will impose constraints on what may be done to them.

Non-physical site features

The locality of the farm, and the proximity to any local marketing outlets, is likely to have a significant influence on the ICM plan. There may be special risks, such as local glasshouses or beekeepers, that will dictate the way in which some weedkillers and insecticides are used. Proximity to a town increases the undesirable problems of vandalism, fly-tipping and theft. This may require special security precautions for buildings and machinery and will affect the choice of fields for theft-prone vegetable crops such as potatoes or brassicas. Climate, especially winter weather, is likely to influence crop and variety choice and the ability to operate machinery. Finally, any special characteristics of the site need to be recorded in the farm survey. For example, is any part of it designated as a Site of Special Scientific Interest, or does it contain any sites of archaeological interest? The farm may be situated in a Nitrate Sensitive Area or in one of the recently designated Nitrate Vulnerable Zones. All of these involve regulations, some voluntary, others mandatory, which may affect farm practices.

Conclusion

Just because the features of the site are more or less fixed does not mean that they should be ignored in determining an ICM plan. Indeed, because they are fixed makes it important to plan a management system that makes best use of them. ICM is site specific and a thorough understanding of the features of the farm is the basis on which all other plans and actions must be determined.

The importance of a site survey

An accurate and detailed farm map is essential in order to make decisions on:

- What is achievable, and what may not be, in an ICM system;

- Where the opportunities lie for improvement;

- Handling special risks (e.g. beehives, fly-tipping etc);

- The cropping plan;

- Management of areas vulnerable to pollution;

- Conservation of wildlife havens and other areas requiring special management input.

3

Crop
Rotation

Introduction

The notion of growing different crops in sequence has long been recognised as an effective means of improving soil fertility and reducing the impact of weeds, insect pests and diseases. The earliest and best known use of the technique was the traditional Norfolk four-course rotation practised at the end of the nineteenth century. This consisted of a sequence of roots (usually turnips or swedes), barley, clover and wheat.

In terms of nutrition, the basic principle of rotation is the alternation of crops like cereals that exhaust the supply of soil nutrients, *(exhaustive crops)* with those that replenish them, such as legumes *(restorative crops)*. Protection against pests is achieved by interrupting the life-cycles of many crop-specific diseases, insects pests and weeds so that, by the time the same crop returns to a field in the rotational sequence, the pest numbers have been severely depleted. The cultivations between crops, particularly where ploughing and burial of surface trash occurred, also helped to prevent the 'carry-over' of some less specific pest problems, while surface cultivation before and after sowing root crops grown in widely spaced rows was useful for controlling troublesome weeds. For this reason, such crops are often referred to as *cleaning crops*.

...benefits of arable rotation

There were, and still are, other benefits from rotational farming. These include the spreading of risk if one crop should fail because of weather, or if market prices for it become depressed, for whatever reason. Equally important is the spread of labour requirements over the year, so that farm staff are kept gainfully occupied. Finally, a rotation allows a balance, in any one year, between crops grown and sold off the farm, known as cash crops, and those used on the farm for feeding livestock so stabilising cash flow and providing the opportunity for the return of nutrients and organic matter to the soil.

The impact of modern technology

With the aid of modern farming practices and technology, many of these benefits can be enjoyed without the need to adhere to a rigid rotation. Farmers have been able to switch from traditional mixed farming to all-arable enterprises consisting entirely of cash crops. This simplification has been made possible by the availability of better machinery for cultivating and harvesting, as well as the technological developments in fertilisers, crop protection products and plant breeding. These have enabled farmers to carry out work on the land more quickly and efficiently which has reduced the need for labour.

Pesticides have provided cost-effective answers to some massively destructive pest problems so increasing yields and income. Plant breeding, too, has made available a wide range of varieties suited to different markets and different growing conditions leading to improved quality and yield. As an added bonus, many varieties also have inbred resistance to some major pest problems (usually diseases). Today we are on the threshold of the introduction of genetically transformed crop varieties which will exhibit properties of insect pest and disease resistance, and even herbicide tolerance, that would have been difficult to achieve by conventional breeding. It remains to be seen whether the promised benefits will become reality, but the prospect is exciting. Finally the various guaranteed price systems for agricultural produce that have operated since the Second World War have helped to even out cash flow over 'good' and 'bad' years.

...continuous cropping

Cereals are the backbone, in financial terms, of UK farming, and the ultimate simplification was to grow them continuously. In the sixties and seventies, on the thinner chalky soils of south-eastern England, many farmers turned to continuous cropping of cereals and became known as the 'barley barons'. Clearly this total abandonment of any form of rotation meant that the natural benefits were lost and had to be replaced artificially. A famous series of experiments at Rothamsted Experimental Station have proved that yields of continuously cropped wheat and barley can be maintained almost indefinitely at a reasonable level if fertiliser input is high enough.

...and problems

But the pendulum had swung far enough. Apart from the huge peaks and troughs in labour demand on the farm, other problems began to emerge. Annual and perennial grass weeds, for example meadow grass, wild oats, blackgrass and couch, thrived under continuous cereal cropping and became a major problem that was only partially answerable with herbicides.

A gradual shift to winter cropping made things worse and brought cereal diseases into prominence. Cereal fungicides initially provided the solution but there was no chemical answer to take-all, and reliance on take-all decline was economically unwise. This meant that the number of wheat crops that could be grown in succession was effectively limited to two.

The control of diseases such as eyespot, mildew and *Septoria*, became totally dependent on one or two chemicals and eventually resistance appeared. Gradually there came a realisation that the traditional benefits of rotation could not be so easily discarded in spite of the advances of technology.

The challenge was to decide what to grow in rotation with the cereals. Potatoes, sugar beet or vining peas and beans were options in some parts of the country and on some soil types. Although the gross margins on many of these crops can be attractive, the capital investment and high variable costs incurred in growing them was often a deterrent. In the livestock areas grass was the obvious choice. More recently, set-aside has been imposed on the rotation. The difficulty was that farmers had trimmed their labour to the bare minimum and were equipped with machinery designed for combinable crops, i.e. those which needed to be sown with a seed drill, harvested with a combine harvester and, perhaps, dried in store.

Salvation came with recognition of the value of oilseed rape in temperate climates and a significantly improved European price support for it. Winter rape fits well as a follow-up to winter barley and can be handled by the normal cereal machinery. The area grown increased rapidly in the late seventies.

Growers of horticultural crops have the same problems. Vegetable growing is highly specialised and intensive. It is a high risk/high return business with success dependant on delivering quality produce at the right time. Often several crops are produced from the same land in one season, resulting in increased risk from some pests and diseases.

Modern rotational farming

Today, even in the most intensive arable systems, some form of alternation of crops is practised. A four-year rotation is now recognised as too short for the effective reduction of some pest problems, and five or six-year sequences are more commonly used. These will nearly always include a succession of two or three cereals between which are grown break crops, one of which is nearly always oilseed rape. Other changes from the original four-course cropping are the replacement of the traditional root crops with potatoes, sugar beet, carrots and, in some parts of the country, mangolds. Beans and peas have replaced red clover or, alternatively, a 2- or 3-year grass ley break is grown. Other oilseed crops, such as linseed and even lupins, have been tried in UK but both present a number of problems which are not associated with oilseed rape.

Rotation and ICM

Integrated Crop Management requires a recognition of the fact that a diverse crop rotation is the most effective indirect means of maintaining soil fertility and controlling pests. By the judicious application of modern technology it seeks to enhance, rather than replace, the benefits of rotation that were apparent 100 years ago. The aim should be to grow healthy, vigorous crops producing economically viable yields and quality by making optimum use of natural resources. In this way the reliance on technological inputs such as fertilisers and pesticides is reduced, but the need for them is by no means eliminated. Such a system also optimises cash flow and makes best use of labour and machinery, just as it did in the nineteenth century.

The actual cropping sequence is central to the whole cropping plan. The most suitable rotation will vary from farm to farm – an indication of why ICM provides guidelines and not prescriptions. Within the cropping sequence consideration must be given to other factors such as the varieties sown, pest control, nutrient availability, environmental impact, harvesting, storage and marketing. A five year rotation is desirable where crops such as sugar beet, potatoes or oilseed rape are involved. Ideally grass leys should be included wherever feasible to improve fertility and build-up soil organic matter. Grass also reduces erosion and prevents nitrogen leaching into groundwater. Demands for labour must also be considered and unmanageable peaks avoided. This would include, for example, the potential conflict of demand for harvesting late winter cereals and drilling oilseed rape.

Finally, from a wildlife viewpoint, a diversity of cropping is important. Furthermore it helps if the various crops are spread around the farm in relatively small units, rather than large blocks, thus creating a mosaic of habitats and a continuity of food supply and shelter within reasonably short distances. This, of course, has to be balanced with the operational advantages of growing larger areas of the same crop in close proximity.

...variety choice

Varieties should be chosen that not only are suited to the climatic and soil characteristics of the farm, but which also meet the requirements of the proposed market. In the modern world, more than ever before, farmers need to be able to meet the demands of their customers. This means identifying in advance what is wanted, and then delivering the product on time to the specification ordered. Plant breeders have produced a wide range of cereal varieties but choice still requires skill. Varieties with a prostrate growth habit help by competing with weeds in the critical early stages of growth. As well as quality, factors such as standing power, drought tolerance and disease resistance all come into the equation. Total reliance on one or two cereal varieties should be avoided in order to minimise the risk if disease resistance should break down. Soon the choice will be widened by the appearance of genetically transformed varieties offering pest resistance, herbicide tolerance or improved agronomic features. Awareness of these developments and being able to fit them into the overall farm cropping plan is an essential part of ICM.

...pest management

Rotation can assist pest control well beyond the choice of resistant varieties. Mention has already been made of the effect of successive cereal crops on the incidence of diseases like take-all and eyespot. There are several other examples where the cropping sequence can encourage pest problems. Where these involve crop-specific problems, such as nematodes in sugar beet or potatoes, the solution is to ensure an adequate interval between repeat cropping on the field. Even on adjacent fields it is sensible to avoid growing the same variety or even the same crop so as to discourage the migration of 'mobile' pest problems from one to the other. These include flying pests, such as aphids, as well as wind-borne fungal spores.

Some problems, such *Sclerotinia*, can affect several crops that might be included in the rotation: in this case oilseed rape, peas, beans, celery and carrots. Awareness of this is clearly important in planning a rotation since growing *any* of these crops in close succession increases the risk from *Sclerotinia*.

In spite of the wide range of available herbicides, some weed problems are still very difficult to control. These include volunteer crop plants, such as potatoes, growing as weeds in other crops. Some grass weeds, such as couch and meadow grasses, can also be difficult to control. More recently the problem of herbicide resistance has arisen, especially with blackgrass which, in some areas, is showing a high level of resistance to many of the products commonly used for its control in cereals. The rotation should provide suitable opportunities for the control of these weeds.

Rotations

1 **Cereals:**
   - Exhaustive (cash) crops;
   - Encourage grass weeds;
   - Continuous cropping encourages take-all, eyespot, nematodes;

2 **Potatoes and root crops:**
   - High value cash crops;
   - Heavy demands for nutrients and labour;
   - Necessary cultivations control many weeds: 'cleaning crops';
   - Continuous cropping very unwise: eelworms;

3 **Pulse crops (e.g. peas and beans):**
   - Cash crops;
   - Natural restoration of nitrogen via bacterial fixation in root nodules;
   - Continuous cropping causes build-up of Sclerotinia, stem rots and eelworms;

4 **Oilseeds (e.g. oilseed rape, linseed):**
   - Cereal break crops;
   - Oilseed rape drilling and harvest fit well into cereal timetable;
   - Thrive on deep soils;
   - Oilseed rape, pulses, sugar beet should not grown on same field more than once in 5 years;

5 **Restorative crops (e.g. leys, kale):**
   - Crops normally fed from the field;
   - Allow return of nutrients and organic matter to soil.

Choosing the right field and measuring environmental impact

Some fields on the farm are likely to be more suitable for particular crops than others. Aspect, topography and soil type need to be taken into account as well as ease of access and possible difficulties operating machinery like combine harvesters. The planned sequence must allow sufficient time for the disposal of any crop residues and the necessary cultivations before drilling or planting the next crop. This means that the cropping plan is likely to include autumn and spring-sown crops. The timing of the cultivations themselves is one of a number of important factors in assessing the environmental impact of the cropping sequence. Damage to the soil structure, disturbance or destruction of nesting sites and removal of food sources can all result from ill-timed cultivation operations. Equally important, the removal of green cover in the autumn months increases the risk of nitrate leaching into groundwater.

...set-aside

Set-aside is now, for most people, an obligatory part of the cropping plan. Set-aside involves taking an area of a farm out of normal arable production in return for payments, provided certain conditions about the management of the set-aside land are fulfilled. Although it has been used in USA since the 1930's, set-aside was first introduced in UK in 1988 as a voluntary measure. The aim was to reduce agricultural production but, although a 10% reduction was achieved in the first year in UK, the effect across the European Union as a whole was negligible. The scheme has been subsequently modified in successive years so that several options are now available and participation is compulsory for all but the smallest holdings in order to qualify for Arable Area Payments on the remainder of the farm.

Although the primary purpose of set-aside is to reduce production, there are considerable secondary benefits which are very much in line with the overall aims of Integrated Crop Management. Rotational set-aside, in particular, has provided an ideal opportunity to control annual and perennial weeds with non-selective herbicides. Set-aside is also an opportunity to reduce inputs and enhance the biodiversity on the farm and there is already evidence that this is happening with bird populations. In choosing which fields are best suited for set-aside, the aims should be to minimise weed seed production and to control perennial weeds and slugs. Top growth needs to be kept to manageable proportions and it is particularly important to avoid harbouring volunteer crops and weeds which act as alternative hosts to diseases or insect pests.

Harvesting and storage

Planning the crop rotation includes considering the requirements for harvesting, storage and marketing the produce. Apart from the obvious need for the correct harvesting machinery and its maintenance, the timing of harvest of the various crops must be matched with the available labour and storage capacity. Some of these factors are very weather dependant and even the best plans can falter, for example in a wet autumn. The plan should allow for this possibility and make alternative provision if necessary.

Pest attack does not stop when the crop is removed from the field and some of the biggest losses to pests occur in store. Whilst there are pesticides available, those used after harvest are the most likely to leave residues on the produce. It is therefore important to include, as part of the overall crop management, measures that will minimise the need for further pesticide use at this stage. This starts with attention to general hygiene in stores and frequent checking of the crops and produce kept in them. Control of ventilation and humidity are essential. Low temperature storage for potatoes and fresh produce helps to maintain it in good condition. In-store traps, such as pheromone traps for saw-toothed grain beetles, give early indications of pest invasion.

Conclusion

The farmers of the late nineteenth century enjoyed the benefits of a managed crop rotation. Integrated Crop Management seeks to combine the best of those traditional practices with modern technology to enhance the advantages for the benefit of farmers and growers, consumers and the environment. By reducing the impact of pests and improving soil health, crop quality is improved, labour management is simplified and cash flow assured. In addition careful planning helps to conserve wildlife havens and enrich general biodiversity on the farm.

Soil Management and Crop Nutrition

Why does the soil need to be managed?

The soil is a living medium and a fundamental natural resource. Careful management is paramount, because without it many of the other inputs to an ICM plan will be negated.

Soil is a dynamic biological system that provides plants with mechanical support, space for root growth and development, oxygen for respiration, water and nutrients for growth and a medium for interaction with other organisms. Soils vary enormously in their natural fertility but in a natural, unmanaged state all soils gradually become more and more acid and the nutrients are depleted.

...replenishing nutrient losses

Whenever any crop is harvested or grazed some of the nutrients used to grow it are taken too. This, of course, includes animal products as well as crops. Additionally, some nutrients, especially nitrogen, are lost to the air or through the soil to groundwater by *leaching*. Even where a large proportion of the nutrients are recycled in the form of farmyard manure or slurry, there is still a net loss of fertility. Nutrient management thus forms an important part of the overall soil management plan.

...optimising the use of available resources

In farming terms, long term experiments have shown that yields obtained without any artificial replenishment of fertility are well under half the optimum yield from a properly managed system. It obviously makes sense, economically and environmentally, to make efficient use of crop and animal wastes, thereby reducing the cost of, and dependence on, manufactured fertilisers. But it is also necessary to adopt farming practices that minimise nutrient losses in the first place, especially where the loss then becomes a pollutant.

...protecting water

Manure or fertiliser in water causes a rapid increase in the population of algae and other higher plants which take advantage of this food supply. In doing so, they use oxygen dissolved in the surface water and, in extreme cases, all the available oxygen can be removed. This enrichment of water by nitrogen or phosphorus is called **eutrophication** and it has a serious effect on water quality.

Other dangers to aquatic life include contaminants such as pesticides or heavy metals which may be present in organic manures, leakage from slurry lagoons and effluent from silage clamps. Storage, maintenance and siting of all these potential sources of pollution needs careful management. The impact clearly depends on the extent of the contamination and the dilution in the water, but sudden inputs can kill large numbers of fish.

Soil management includes calculations of the risk of run-off from the land into watercourses. The speed at which soils soak up liquid is important in working out this risk. Water ponding on the soil is a clear indication that it is being applied (whether as rainfall or by the grower) faster than it can be absorbed, and the risk of run-off is clearly heightened, especially on sloping ground. Paradoxically, fields with effective land drainage systems create a particular risk because of the higher speed at which liquids can reach watercourses.

The potential for damage, in a badly managed system, to watercourses and the life they support is therefore considerable.

Planning for better soil management

Planning soil management starts with a detailed knowledge of the soil on the farm which should be assembled by creating a soil map. This is information that is specific to the site and it is one of the fundamental reasons why ICM can never be a prescriptive set of rules.

The MAFF *Code of Good Agricultural Practice for the Protection of Soil* is a practical guide to help farmers and growers avoid causing long-term damage to their soils. It also provides general guidance on practices which will maintain the ability of the soil to support plant growth.

...finding out about the soil on the farm

Ideally farmers need to be able to identify their main *soil series* because these are groupings of soils that respond to management in a consistent and predictable way. Each soil series is given a name, normally that of a place near where it is commonly found and usually where it was first recognised and described. For example, the Evesham series are lime-rich soils formed from clays and found in Warwickshire, Gloucestershire, Somerset and the East and West Midlands. They are normally very heavy soils best suited to grass and cereals.

Professional advice is available, but there are also soil maps available from which farms can identify the soil series likely to be present on their land. There are about six most likely to be present, and the top 38 series cover 80% of the farmland in England and Wales.

...making a farm soil map

An accurate map provides site-specific information about the soil's water holding capacity, its workability, drainage and waterlogging, acidity and natural fertility. More refined mapping techniques can provide information to show how quickly nutrients and chemicals can leach through the soil. The map forms the basis of an action plan.

Soils vary from field to field, and often within fields. The scale of the map may be governed by the size of the farm but a sampling frequency of one point for every 2ha of land is a workable guideline. From what has been said it is clear that the map should contain qualitative and quantitative information covering such things as textures and pH, structure, organic matter content, top soil depth and areas which will require special treatment, perhaps because of the presence of pans or impermeable layers.

...soil fauna and flora

Soil life is abundant and diverse. It contains not only visible organisms such as earthworms and a variety of soil living insects, but also literally millions of micro-organisms. These include nematodes, algae, fungi, protozoa and bacteria. Estimates of the mass of microbes in soil range from 800 to 3000kg dry weight per hectare in the top 20 cm of soil. Not all soil organisms are beneficial and the abundance of those that are pests, such as nematodes, is heavily influenced by cropping rotation.

Other factors that can have a bearing on soil populations are soil type, temperature, water supply, the concentration of some heavy metals and the use of pesticides.

Soil fauna and flora

"It has been estimated that there are one billion bacteria, one thousand metres of fungi and thousands of tiny animals and algae in a thimbleful of fertile soil. This is equivalent to one tonne of microbes per hectare of soil."
Bill Butterworth

Micro-organisms play a vital role in maintaining soil health by processing (*mineralising*) organic matter to liberate nutrients for use by growing plants. The process produces humus which contributes to creating the soil structure.

Clearly a soil management plan must aim to integrate maintenance of the physical structure with protection of the fauna and flora. A single act of cultivation may be as damaging to the latter as it is beneficial to the former.

...defining texture

In addition to the fertility status of soil, its physical *texture* is also vitally important. All soils consist of a mixture of different sized particles which are classed as sand, silt or clay, according to their size, together with organic matter and a variety of soil-living creatures. The amount of organic matter in mineral soils is typically 0.5 – 2.5%, but on fen or peat soils the proportion can be as high as 40 – 50%. At these levels the behaviour of the soil, and in particular the capacity to adsorb chemicals, is significantly changed. Also, although rich in nitrogen, black fen soils are generally deficient in other essential crop nutrients.

Field determination of soil texture

By rubbing a moist sample of soil between thumb and fingers it is possible to classify the texture of the soil according to the 'feel' of the dominant particles:

Clay is sticky, will take a polish and forms a ball that can be moulded with difficulty;

Silt feels silky and smooth, will take a slight polish and forms a cohesive ball that can be easily moulded;

Sand feels gritty and can be heard if rubbed close to the ear; it forms a less cohesive ball that is easily deformed.

Soil particles are classified into categories according to their size:

Material	Particle diameter
Clay	<0.002 mm
Silt	0.02 – 0.002 mm
Sand	2.0 – 0.02 mm

The texture of a soil depends on the relative proportions of the different particles and organic matter. There is a relatively simple method by which a competent advisor can determine soil texture using the MAFF *Soil Texture (85) System*. This can influence decisions about pesticide choice and dose. Texture is also a guide to the ease of cultivation of a soil.

...the importance of soil structure

Soil structure is the result of the way in which soil particles aggregate together. It depends on all the properties (mentioned above) that determine texture, together with chemical factors and the activity of organisms such as earthworms. The structure of a soil has a major influence on the ease with which water and air move about in it, and on moisture retention. These factors affect crop growth and the availability of nutrients but they also influence what happens in periods of very dry or very wet weather. A normal arable soil is regularly cultivated to a depth of 20-30 cm which is the main area for crop root development, although most crops can develop roots well below this level for the uptake of water and nutrients. Problems occur on some soils if a crop is established at a time of plentiful supply of water and nutrients in the surface layers. Root growth develops only in these layers and may not be sufficiently deep to cope with later drought conditions.

Improving the physical condition of the soil

Maintenance or improvement of the soil structure is an essential part of any farming system. The physical condition of the soil is most affected by cultivation techniques, machines and soil water management. The MAFF *Codes of Good Agricultural Practice* for soil, water and air, together with the SOAFD *Code of Good Agricultural Practice for the Prevention of Environmental Pollution from Agricultural Activity* all give valuable guidance.

...matching resources to needs

It is self-evident that the amount of work that can be done is limited by the number of available work days and the available manpower. However, it is much better to estimate these in advance and plan ahead, rather than discovering where the bottleneck occurs in mid-season. The plan should not only schedule the work to be done, but it should also be a strategy for minimisation of damage to the soil structure. There are various measures that can be taken to achieve this including matching tractor power to the job and using special equipment such as dual wheels, flotation tyres or tracks. Regular maintenance of all vehicles, with particular attention to tyre pressures is an integral part of the overall plan.

Field operations must be matched to the crop and the prevailing soil conditions. This involves actually measuring soil moisture and compaction by digging a hole with a spade and examining the exposed profile for evidence of compaction or a plough pan. From these measurements and the weather forecast, decisions can be made about the best time and method for cultivation. Here, as with everything in ICM, there is no hard and fast rule to follow, and sometimes different aims will make conflicting demands. For example, non-inversion cultivations require less energy than ploughing and do less damage to the soil fauna. On the other hand, this will encourage annual grass weeds and it is less beneficial than ploughing if the structure needs to be improved. An Integrated Crop Management system means exactly that: all needs must be considered, and the eventual action should be the result of a balanced assessment. In this case it is likely that the best course will be alternate ploughing and non-inversion techniques in the rotation.

...soil water management

Soil water management is concerned with the conservation of moisture at certain times, its removal at others and the prevention of soil erosion. The two main factors involved in erosion are wind and water, and the extent of the problem varies according to soil type, location, slope, field size and crop husbandry. In severe cases erosion can lead to substantial crop losses and water pollution. The measures necessary to prevent this on any farm will vary, but the overriding principle should be to avoid leaving the soil bare. In some countries there is a legal requirement to have green cover of some sort during the autumn months. This is not the case in UK, but nevertheless it is a sound principle. The timely establishment of autumn crops not only stabilises the soil during the wet winter months, but it also plays an important part in preventing nitrogen leaching. Leaving an uncultivated grassy buffer strip alongside watercourses assists in avoiding direct pollution by fertiliser or pesticides, but it also protects the water from direct run-off or wash-down of soil.

Heavy metals in soil

Maximum permitted concentrations (mg/kg dry matter) of metals in soil after application of sewage sludge

Soil pH				
Metal	5.0–5.5	5.5–6.0	6.0–7.0	>7.0
Zinc	200	250	300	450
Copper	80	100	135	200
Nickel	50	60	75	110

Source: MAFF *Code of Good Agricultural Practice for the Protection of Soil*

Organic manures are a valuable means of building up soil organic matter which assists water retention and protects against erosion. However, liquid organic wastes require special care in order to avoid soil pollution from the possible presence of heavy metals, and by nitrate leaching. This risk is higher from animal manures and organic wastes than it is from inorganic fertilisers. Nitrogen application should never exceed the crop requirements and the maximum amount of nitrogen from organic manure should be 250kg per hectare in any year. On sloping land or near domestic properties where there is a risk of water or air pollution, organic manures should be incorporated into the soil as soon as they are spread.

Crop nutrition management

Plants depend on mineral nutrients for their growth and development. There are 13 elements (see table) which are essential for all plant growth and a further four or five which are beneficial for some plants.

The six major nutrients are nitrogen, phosphorus, potassium, sulphur, calcium and magnesium. The first three of these are required in the largest amounts and are normally referred to colloquially by their chemical symbols N, P and K, although they are always utilised as compounds of these elements. Plants can only take up these nutrients as water soluble compounds and it is often the case that while the topsoil content of nitrogen may be relatively high, only a small proportion is available following release in a complex web of interrelated biological and chemical breakdown. This is known as *the nitrogen cycle*.

Plant nutrients

Nutrient and symbol	Form in which taken up by plants	Removal by 5t/ha @ 20% m.c (kg/ha)
Macronutrients		
Nitrogen (N)	NH_4^+, NO_3^-	105
Phosphorus (P)	$H_2PO_4^-$	18
Potassium (K)	K^+	15
Sulphur (S)	SO_4^{--}	8
Magnesium (Mg)	Mg^{++}	6
Calcium (Ca)	Ca^{++}	2
Trace elements		
Chlorine (Cl)	Cl^-	3
Iron (Fe)	Fe^{++}	0.2
Manganese (Mn)	Mn^{++}	0.2
Zinc (Zn)	Zn^{++}	0.2
Copper (Cu)	Cu^{++}	0.03
Boron (B)	H_3BO_3	0.02
Molybdenum (Mo)	$M_0O_4^{--}$	–

Source: IAEA

...nitrogen

Nitrogen is taken up by plants in a number of ways. Soil organic matter and crop residues are broken down by microbial conversion to soluble forms in a process known as **mineralisation**. This process occurs whenever the soil is not frozen and in the UK is most rapid in autumn when soils are warm and moist. A second source of nitrogen is obtained from the atmosphere by a bacterial process known as **nitrogen fixation** in which it is made available as nitrate or ammonia. Thirdly, nitrogen is obtained from soluble organic compounds such as urea and amino acids, whether from animals or applied as fertiliser. Finally, these sources of nitrogen can be supplemented by manufactured nitrogen fertiliser.

The rate at which crops take up nitrogen varies with the crop, its rate of growth and stage of development. Some crops like cereals have a peak demand during early growth while others, for example potatoes, have a more even uptake during the season. However, care is necessary in treating a backward cereal crop. Although the demand may be high, the ability to take up a heavy nitrogen dressing may be limited by a root-system that is not yet well-developed. In such cases split treatments may have to be considered.

Highly permeable underlying rock like sandstone or limestone will allow rapid movement of excess nitrate through to groundwater. This has led to the creation of a voluntary scheme of restriction of nitrogen use in UK (Nitrate Sensitive Areas) and proposed statutory areas of control (Nitrate Vulnerable Zones) under the EC Nitrate Directive. This Directive requires restrictions in any area with 'polluted' water, which is defined as any surface or groundwater that contains, or could contain, more than 50 mg nitrate per litre if action is not taken.

Nitrate Sensitive Areas (NSAs):

- Voluntary scheme covering 32 specified areas in England and Wales on sandstone, limestone or chalk where nitrate contamination of drinking water deemed most likely to occur. Farmers join scheme for 5 years and adopt restrictions on nitrogen inputs, crop cover and organic manures;

- Premium scheme involves higher payments for converting from arable to grass;

- Administered by MAFF;

- Scheme covered 19,600 hectares by 1996.

Nitrate Vulnerable Zones:

- Proposed statutory controls designed to achieve much the same result as NSA scheme;

- Requirements largely in line with 'best practice' and *Code of Good Agricultural Practice for the Protection of Water*;

- Manufactured N banned between 1 September and 1 February unless there is a specific crop need;

- Organic manure total quantities limited;

- Field by field records of N usage compulsory;

- MAFF grant of 25% available for providing facilities to separate clean and dirty water.

The ultimate result of nitrate loss to groundwater is the contamination of drinking water supplies where the EC Drinking Water Directive also imposes a maximum nitrate concentration of 50 mg per litre.

...the right nutrients in the right amounts at the right time

Like everything else in Integrated Crop Management, crop nutrition requires planning. Crops need an adequate supply of food and it is clear that, in any seasonal sequence of cropping, the natural fertility of the soil must be supplemented to achieve optimum results. Even soils like light sandy soils, which have low natural nutrient reserves, can be highly productive when managed properly. In an ICM system the aims should be to make best use of the natural resources and then to supplement them by using the right nutrients in the right amounts in the right place. This demands skill and often professional advice.

The starting point in making the best use of resources is to devise a cropping and soil care strategy that minimises unnecessary nutrient losses. This will include maintaining green cover on the land, especially in the autumn months and keeping cultivations to the minimum. After ploughing in high-residue crops, such as grass, it is important to make sure that the subsequent crop is established quickly to utilise the high nutrient release from the decaying grass before it is lost in the lower levels of the soil and ultimately to watercourses.

...nutrient status

The **nutrient status** of the soil needs to be determined at the outset and then repeated every 3–5 years. This includes a measurement of acidity (pH) as well as levels of phosphorus, potassium and magnesium.

The **nitrogen index** of the soil (on a scale of 0 – 2) is based on the previous crop grown in the field. The higher indices are achieved after crops that have received large quantities of nitrogen fertiliser, such as permanent pasture and potatoes, or have created large reserves of nitrogen, such as legumes. Crops like cereals, maize and forage crops, that are removed from the field, generally result in a Nitrogen Index of 0. Mineral nitrogen analysis helps in the diagnosis and prevention of nutritional disorders in crops. For arable soils samples should be taken with a screw auger to a depth of about 15 cm (6"). At least 25 sub-samples should be taken from each sampling area (about

6 hectares (15 acres)), bulked and sent to a specialist laboratory offering an analysis service.

Nitrogen, phosphorus and potassium are the major elements whose levels would gradually decrease without replenishment and, assuming satisfactory levels to start with, the aim must be to replace that which is removed so that the nutrient status is maintained.

...supply and demand

Farm requirements are worked out by calculating a 'balance sheet' of supply and demand. Predicted demand needs to be based on a realistic yield projection, the current state of the crop and its variety, and the seasonal weather. Supply is calculated from information about previous cropping (the Nitrogen Index), the status of other nutrients and the contribution from any organic manuring. Fertiliser needs to make up the balance can then be calculated.

Whilst some of the judgements must be subjective, they should be based on what is already known. This includes information from the farm soil map, past yields and experience, and rainfall data. Clearly, the more complete these records are, the sounder will be the decisions made. Additional help and guidance is available in publications from MAFF and fertiliser manufacturers. This includes, for example, nitrogen indices and information on the composition and nutrient value of different animal manures and crop wastes. The MAFF *Reference Book 209 Fertiliser Recommendations for Agricultural and Horticultural Crops* is an essential companion for the calculation of detailed fertiliser requirements.

Using fertilisers: choice, type and quality

Fertiliser is either natural or manufactured. Choice of which type to use will, to some extent, be governed by the availability of organic manures from the farm enterprise. These may include farmyard manure, slurry, sewage sludge, crop residues and green manures. Their quality and availability will vary from farm to farm and from year to year. They are nevertheless a valuable resource requiring careful management to ensure that they remain a benefit and do not become a pollutant.

Fertiliser choice

Natural		Manufactured	
Natural	• FYM; • Slurry; • Sewage sludge; • Crop residues; • Green manure.	**Manufactured**	• Solid: straight; compound; • Liquid.

It is important to provide safe storage capacity with protection against overspill. A farm waste management plan (see chapter 6) further helps to minimise this risk. The nutrient value of organic manures needs to be determined so as to make full allowance for them in the fertiliser plan.

...manufactured fertiliser

Manufactured fertilisers may be solid or liquid and the former group may be *single* or *straight* (i.e. supplying one major nutrient, usually nitrogen) or *compound*, a mixture of various nutrients in differing proportions designed to meet the typical needs of specific crops. Liquid fertilisers are transported, delivered and stored in bulk, whilst solids may be handled in bulk or in bags. The first step is to choose a good quality product.

Solid fertilisers vary hugely in their quality and the difficulties in handling inferior products may quickly outweigh any cost savings in their purchase. A good quality fertiliser needs to be free flowing and consist of even sized particles (ideally 2 – 4 mm) that do not shatter in use. A measure of quality is given in the spread pattern (SP) rating and products with a high rating should be chosen. 'SP5' is top grade.

...storage and handling

All fertilisers will deteriorate unless properly stored. Additionally, they are valuable commodities and some are a fire risk. Responsible storage, considering the needs of both operator and environmental safety, is important. Stores should be secure against unauthorised entry and both buildings and vehicles should carry the appropriate hazard signs for transport. Ammonium nitrate should not be stored with other combustible materials.

Storage of fertiliser

Detailed guidance on the storage of fertilisers is give in *The Health and Safety Handbook* published by the Fertiliser Manufacturers Association. Key points are:

- Stores should not be located near hospitals, schools etc, or potential sources of fire;

- Fertiliser should not be stored where it can become affected by heat or mixed with combustible materials;

- Urea and ammonium nitrate based fertilisers should be stored separately;

- The top of stacks or heaps should be at least 1 metre below eaves, beams and light fittings;

- Bags should be stacked in stable heaps on level, well-drained ground.

Transporting ammonium nitrate

Most fertilisers are subject to national and international transport regulations with particular reference to the hazards of handling ammonium nitrate. There are some exceptions, but the general rules are:

- All vehicles should be diesel powered;

- Drivers of vehicles >3.5 tonnes must have special training;

- Drivers carrying loads of over 500kg in packages greater than 25kg must abide by the transport regulations;

- Drivers must carry documents indicating the nature and danger of the goods, safety measures, first aid measures, fire-fighting requirements and measures to be taken in the case of deterioration of packages;

- Vehicles must display an orange hazard warning rectangle when loaded. It **must** be removed when the load is removed;

- The regulations do not apply when no more than 10 tonnes are carried on an agricultural vehicle over no more than 12 km between land occupied by the same farmer.

Note: This is an outline of the regulations which are covered in *Dangerous Goods: An Operator's Guide* published by the Freight Transport Association.

The MAFF *Code of Good Agricultural Practice for the Protection of Water (COGAPP)* is an essential source of guidance not only on the storage, but also the use of fertilisers. Managers and operators need to be familiar with these guidelines so that, for example, solid fertilisers are not stored close to field drains or watercourses, where leakage is likely to lead to prosecution and a fine.

...proper machinery operation

A fertiliser spreader is a precision tool and yet a survey has shown that over half of those in use in UK are never calibrated and a similar proportion of operators have never seen the machine manual. One of the practical difficulties here is that there generally has to be gross inaccuracy in application before an effect can be seen in the crop, and then it may be weeks, or even months, after the event. But damage does not have to be visible, and a uniformly green crop does not necessarily indicate optimum use of fertiliser.

...calibrating

Achieving a uniform spread pattern can be tricky and requires attention to detail. At the top of the list is training of the operator and regular maintenance of the machine. Next comes calibration, and this should be done with all the products to be used. Settings for each product can be noted to reduce (but not eliminate) the setting- up procedure later. Spread patterns can be checked using trays, but the height recommended by the manufacturer for the required working width needs to be set in the field. This is because running in deeply rutted tramlines affects the working height above the crop.

...before starting

Weather conditions are important. Wet and windy conditions should be avoided as should applying to, or travelling on, waterlogged, frozen or snow-covered ground. Ringing the local weather centre can provide an accurate forecast for the ensuing twelve hours and is worth the effort if there is any doubt about whether to start a task.

...in the field

During application the machine performance should be continually monitored. Spreading on headlands, water buffer zones and in hedge bottoms and ditches must be avoided and this can be helped by the use of devices on the spreading equipment, such as deflectors, tilts and cut-offs, all of which assist in achieving accurate placement in these vulnerable areas. In the body of the field, care is necessary to maintain the bout width, forward speed and flow rate. If necessary, consideration should be given to altering rates to meet special needs. If contractors are used for fertiliser spreading, they should be acquainted with the overall farm strategy and their work should be monitored to check that they comply.

The FACTS scheme

Accurate determination of crop nutrition requirements is complex and needs to take account of a number of factors. Furthermore the ability of a crop to use up the available nitrogen depends on many factors, so requirements will not be the same from crop to crop nor from field to field. Good advice is vital.

The Fertiliser Advisors Certification and Training Scheme (FACTS) is designed to ensure the competence and professionalism of those giving advice on the use of fertilisers in the field. It is administered by BASIS, who also run a similar scheme for crop protection advisors. Advisors are required to undergo training followed by an examination before they are awarded a certificate of competence. Growers then have the assurance that advisors carrying a FACTS card have demonstrated that they have the experience and competence to give sound advice. If professional advice is needed – and, on crop nutrition matters, it usually is – always choose a FACTS qualified supplier or consultant.

Conclusion

The soil is a major natural resource for any horticultural or farming enterprise but it is frequently abused or neglected. Correct management is an essential element of ICM. Fertiliser choice, application and timing is one of the most vital inputs and yet is one of the least precisely controlled. A planned fertiliser strategy is economically and environmentally beneficial. Taking qualified professional advice and using good quality products will help to ensure that the right nutrients are applied in the right amounts in the right place at the right time. Achievement of this will underpin all other ICM strategies.

Crop
Protection

Protection against what?

Cultivated land left unattended will quickly grow a variety of plant life. Although seemingly haphazard, this invasion by plants is strictly self-regulated. The plants that appear will not be all of the same type, nor will they grow in straight lines. Some individuals will survive at the expense of others. Prostrate species become intermingled with more erect plants so that not only does the soil surface become fully utilised, but so too is the space for several centimetres above it.

In this way nature exploits all the available living space, or niches. The species that grow first are those best adapted to occupy these niches and best able to compete for the available sources of nutrient, light and water. Collectively they are called **weeds** - plants growing where they are not wanted. The density and composition of the weed population will be governed by a whole range of factors such as previous cropping, nutrient availability and soil acidity.

Pests and Crops

- Most weeds grow very quickly and are prolific seed producers;

- Weeds compete vigorously for nutrients, light and water;

- Crop yields and quality suffer when invaded by weeds therefore control is essential;

- Other organisms, such as eelworms, insects, fungi, rodents and birds, invade crops and damage them;

- All organisms that hamper man's efforts to grow crops are termed *pests*;

- Pest invasion of crops is inevitable because *monoculture* leaves biological gaps, or *niches*, available for them to occupy.

A cultivated field sown with a crop, all of the same type, all germinating at the same time and all growing to the same height, is very different to this natural state. **Monoculture** is a man-made system sometimes likened to a housing estate with only half the properties inhabited. It is obvious that the available niches are not fully occupied, and nature's squatters quickly start filling the gaps. Weed species arrive, and, because they are vigorous competitors, they will grow at the expense of the sown crop. The result is that, at best, the yield and quality of the crop suffers or, at worst, it is completely wiped out, while at the same time the weeds flourish and deposit huge reserves of seed into the soil ready to compete with the next crop sown.

Weed invasion into cultivated crops is therefore inevitable and control is usually essential.

Other organisms also invade crops. These may range from bacteria, or even viruses, to soil-living eelworms, flying or crawling insects, fungal diseases and higher animals such as rodents and birds. The presence of at least some of these in a monoculture is as inevitable as the presence of weeds. If they live on the crop and use it as a food source, they will cause damage and, along with weeds, they need to be controlled.

For convenience, organisms, whether weeds, insects, animals or diseases, that damage crops are collectively described as **pests**. The chemicals that are used to control them are therefore called pesticides, whether they are weedkillers, or products to control insects or diseases. Crop protection is the science of controlling pests safely, effectively and economically, not just by using chemical control measures, but by considering **all** the available options. Indeed, the best exponents of ICM are those who optimise the use of non-chemical methods but integrate the judicious use of pesticides where necessary.

Crop protection in ICM

It is not sufficient merely to accept the inevitable presence of pests that must be dealt with as they appear. Economically this would be unwise in any system, but ICM demands that farmers and growers adopt a structured and long-term approach to pest control. Prevention is always better then cure, but if this is not possible, the cure must take account of the overall aims of ICM to balance economic production with environmental sensitivity.

Crop protection and ICM

- Prevention is better than cure;

- Prevention is sometimes possible and cure is not always necessary;

- Cure must balance economic production with environmental sensitivity;

- Pest control strategy should keep pests below economically damaging levels and use the best combination of available control methods;

- Crop protection in an ICM system must be structured, long-term and involve the whole farm.

Pest *prevention* is sometimes possible, while *cure* may not always be necessary. Those who practise ICM should aim to devise a management strategy to keep pest levels below economically damaging thresholds by using the most appropriate combination of biological, cultural, mechanical and chemical methods. The process involves:
- Planning;
- Evaluation of non-chemical pest reduction strategies;
- Pest prediction and identification;
- Use of rotations;
- Choice of most appropriate pesticide and its application;
- Keeping records.

Planning

Those who start considering pest control only when they see the pest (or, more likely, the damage it has caused) will never succeed. Like all living organisms, pests thrive in some circumstances and struggle to survive in others. Just as one swallow does not make a summer, so one aphid does not make an infestation that requires treatment. Some pests are a greater threat to one crop than to another or they may be suited to particular soils or climates. Presence of a pest (especially a weed) in one year is a good (but not totally reliable) indication of invasion in the following year, or, perhaps, when the same crop is next grown in the field.

Planning starts with understanding the farm, its history and its crops. Awareness of the pests likely to appear and their economic threshold levels is an essential first step. Rotations and choice of pest and disease resistant varieties can do much to reduce the chances of pest damage long before the crop is ever sown. Keeping up-to-date with technological progress in pest control is a continuous process. Those practising ICM keep a special look-out for developments, such as satellite mapping or genetically engineered pest-resistant crops, which may reduce or replace the use of chemical pesticides.

Finally, the planning stage includes maintenance of the equipment that will be used to apply pesticides, together with training of the staff who operate it. Methods of storage and disposal of chemical pesticides, including the emergency procedures for dealing with accidents, should be reviewed and updated.

Planning

- Don't wait for the pests;
- Create a long-term strategy taking account of past history and present cropping;
- Be aware of what pests may appear and their economic thresholds;
- Adjust rotations and variety choice if necessary;
- Keep up-to-date with developments;
- Maintain equipment and train staff;
- Review storage, disposal and accident procedures.

Evaluation of non-chemical pest reduction strategies

In any farming system, total reliance on chemical pest control is unwise, and unlikely to succeed. By definition, pests are adaptable organisms. Over the 50 years since chemical pesticides began to be used on any scale, there have been numerous instances of resistance, sometimes leading to widescale control failures and changes in control practice. Examples of this are the resistance of the peach-potato aphid (*Myzus persicae*) to organophosphorus insecticides, and the rapid spread of resistance to mbc-fungicides in cereal eyespot (*Pseudocercosporella herpotrichoides*).

Pests have natural enemies and, as indicated above, have climatic and host preferences. By exploiting these features much can be done to reduce the incidence, spread and impact of pest species long before chemical control needs to be contemplated. Indeed, careful management of the non-chemical options can sometimes eliminate the need for further control measures, although some degree of chemical pest control is usually necessary.

There are a number of non-chemical options that should be considered in an ICM system.

...crop rotation

Surveys have shown that the composition of weed populations is largely unaffected by annual cropping sequences – in general the same weed species are likely to appear each year regardless of the crop being grown unless a switch is made to a perennial crop like grass. However, the **abundance** of some species can be greatly influenced by crop rotation. For example, continuous runs of cereals are likely to result in a build-up of grass weeds, especially blackgrass and wild oats. Some of these are, however, significantly influenced by cultivation practices (see below), so an option exists to reduce them by other means.

Insect and disease pests are different. They get their food from the crop plants, not from the soil, and very often they have specific preferences in this regard. Their incidence is therefore dependant on the presence of a suitable host crop. This is why growing successive crops of winter wheat results in a build-up of eyespot and take-all, and a break from this crop is an effective non-chemical means of reducing these pests. Some pests such as eelworms or *Sclerotinia* disease (oilseed rape, peas, beans) or white rot (onions, leeks) can survive in soil for several years and attack when the host crop is planted again.

In all these cases awareness of the problems and carefully planned rotations incorporating suitably long breaks between host crops can do much to reduce pest incidence.

...attention to farm hygiene

Annual weeds spread by seed. The soil carries a huge 'bank' of weed seeds some of which can survive in a dormant state for several years until favourable conditions for germination and growth occur. Indeed, this is one of the characteristics of a successful weed species. The only way to reduce this seed burden in the field is by a slow war of attrition, but a key to success is to reduce as far as possible any return of additional seed to the bank. This means not only attending to the control of the weeds within the crop, but making sure that weeds elsewhere on the farm, on non-cropped land, on roadways and round the buildings are not allowed to flower and set seed.

While some insect and disease pests live in the soil in the field, many do not. These invade crops from outside. Obviously little can be done about invasion of flying insects or wind-borne spores from neighbouring farms, counties or even continents. However, the risk can be greatly reduced by eliminating sources of infection or infestation on the farm. For example, diseases such as take-all use weed grasses as alternative hosts. Potato clamps and dumps are the most usual farm infection focus for potato blight, and good hygiene, including prompt destruction of any spring growth, is an essential component of control.

...use of resistant varieties

Sometimes the host preference of a pest relates to a particular variety or group of varieties. This can occur because of some natural difference, such as hairiness or leaf wax. More usually it is because some varieties have an inbred resistance (or tolerance) to the pest, normally fungal diseases. Conventional plant breeding is, however, a slow process, and it takes a long time to combine a range of desirable attributes (which must also include yield and quality factors) in one plant. It is rare for a variety to carry effective resistance to more than two or three of the major diseases that may attack it.

In order to make best use of the varieties available, it is therefore vital to be aware of the particular disease risks on the farm before deciding which varieties to grow. It is equally important to keep informed about new varieties.

Genetic engineering may soon change the whole scene. New transgenic crop varieties can be produced much more quickly than by conventional breeding, and, provided the appropriate genes can be found, it may well be possible to combine specific insect or disease resistances with tolerance to a herbicide. These developments are still in their infancy but nevertheless they should be watched.

...cultivations

All pests must survive the winter somewhere. Weeds do so as seeds in the soil. Insect pests generally take shelter on an alternative host but some also move down into the soil. Fungal diseases either produce resting bodies which fall to the soil, or they survive on dead and decaying organic matter, or they live on autumn sown crops – the 'green bridge'.

In all these cases it is clear that management of the soil can play a key part in non-chemical pest control. Nothing survives burial indefinitely. For example, wild oat seeds can survive for many years buried in soil, but they will not germinate unless brought back to the surface layers. Eyespot disease of cereals can survive on the base of the stems in a stubble, but is eliminated by deep burial. However, the benefits of ploughing must be set against the possible disadvantages. For example, on heavy soils, ploughing can lead to cloddy seedbeds which may not suit the crop, will hinder herbicide performance and may encourage slugs.

Some weeds germinate mainly (but unfortunately never exclusively) at a particular time of year. For example, blackgrass and cleavers mostly appear in the autumn. Where this occurs the 'stale seedbed' technique (cultivating and then leaving time for weeds to germinate before killing them with a further cultivation before drilling) can achieve major reductions before the crop is even sown. Similarly, research has shown that delayed drilling of autumn sown cereals significantly reduces the likelihood of infection by some fungal diseases.

...biological control

There are few animal organisms that do not have natural enemies. This notion is implicit in the fundamental concept of food chains. Similarly, the vast majority of the world's insects feed on plants. It follows that isolation and exploitation of the natural enemies of pest organisms is a non-chemical control option that must be considered. However, there are practical limitations to any system of biological control.

Firstly, the system is self-regulating. The predator cannot survive without the presence of the victim - the pest organism -which may well have caused damage to the crop before it is itself killed. Secondly, as the pest population decreases so must the numbers of predators. The populations of each track each other in a cyclical manner in which neither is totally eliminated. The result is that the degree, duration and reliability of control achievable in a biological system is normally inferior to that obtained with chemicals.

Nevertheless, there are opportunities for biological control, particularly in glasshouse crops, where there may not be suitable chemical products. The majority of commercialisations so far have been products for the control of insects, with the bacterium *Bacillus thuringiensis* (*Bt*) a leading example. *Bt* controls caterpillars in brassicas, vegetables, soft fruit and ornamentals. Other examples in use in UK are *Encarsia formosa*, a parasitic wasp for control of whitefly in glasshouses, and the fast-moving predatory mite *Phytoseiulus persimilis* for red spider mite control in glasshouses. *Verticillium lecanii* is a fungal parasite used to control aphids and whitefly in protected crops, and *Trichoderma viride* is an example of the control of a fungal disease (Silver Leaf in plums) by a fungal parasite.

Biological control of weeds is not yet a realistic option although considerable work has been done on the use of caterpillars and flea beetles for the control of ragwort.

...encouragement of natural predators

Many pests, but especially aphids, have natural predators, such as ladybirds and parasitic wasps, living with them in the crop and the immediate surroundings. These predators themselves cannot adequately reduce a heavy pest invasion, but they make a significant contribution. Measures to encourage them therefore form an important part of an ICM pest control strategy.

If they are managed correctly, the margins of arable fields provide ample havens for these predators, some of which are known to have host preferences. For example, *Phacelia tanacetifolia* is favoured by the hoverfly predators of aphids. There can be problems with very large fields because it can take predators, many of which are flightless, a long time to reach the middle. In these cases, a simple alternative method of encouraging these predators is to create mid-field refuges, or 'beetle banks', from where they can easily spread across a crop.

An additional benefit from the creation of species-rich field margins is a general increase in the supply of insect food and seeds for birds (see Wildlife and Landscape Management).

...other considerations

For some weed problems, for example roguing light infestations of wild oats, manual labour should be considered, but the number of cases where this is both an economic and effective option will be few.

Pest control does not end when the crop is harvested. Indeed, for many crops the greatest losses to pests occur in store at a time when there are far fewer chemical options and when chemical treatments are least desirable. In these circumstances, careful attention to store hygiene and environmental control is essential.

Evaluation of other options

- Never rely entirely on chemical pest control;

- Crop rotations are an essential means of reducing the impact of many insect and disease pests, and some weeds;

- Farm hygiene helps prevent replenishment of the soil 'seed bank' and delays appearance of some insects and diseases;

- Resistant varieties are useful if they also meet the commercial requirements of yield and quality;

- Cultural methods such as burial by ploughing, delayed drilling or use of stale seedbeds can help reduce some pests;

- Biological control opportunities are generally limited to glasshouse crops;

- Consider using manual labour.

Pest prediction

Forewarned is forearmed. Of all pests, the incidence of weeds is least affected by outside influences. Previous experience and existing records will be a reliable guide to the species that will normally appear and plans should be made accordingly. Predictions should always be confirmed by regular field inspections and maintenance of weed maps will aid decisions in future seasons.

Pest prediction

- Forewarned is forearmed;

- Experience and records, including maps, are especially useful for forecasting weed infestations;

- Long- and short-term weather forecasts will give a good prediction of invasion by some pests;

- Take note of official warnings (eg for potato blight, apple mildew, sugar beet aphids).

By contrast, insect pests and diseases are much more influenced by weather conditions. For example, cutworms and aphid pests like greenfly and blackfly generally flourish in hot, dry summers; yellow rust disease of wheat spreads in cool humid conditions; snow rot disease of barley favours, as its name implies, cold moist weather following a covering of snow.

Awareness of these conditions clearly assists in predicting pest attack and this should be backed up by taking note of long-range and short-term weather forecasts. In addition, official warnings are issued when weather conditions have favoured the spread of problems such as potato blight, apple mildew or sugar beet aphids.

Computerised models can be used to predict some pest problems and this area of technology is soon likely to produce some sophisticated decision support systems.

Identification and evaluation

Having predicted what pests may appear, correct identification is the next step. Even more important is an evaluation of whether the infestation merits treatment. Total control is rarely needed and treatment thresholds must always be considered.

Weeds are static and relatively easy to identify using the various books and guides that are available, or by using a competent BASIS registered advisor. Nevertheless it is important to do this as soon as the weeds are seen. Weeds get more difficult to control as they grow larger which may mean using a higher dose than would have been the case with prompt action. Furthermore, as long as they remain untreated they are competing with the crop for light, water and nutrients.

Insect pests present a bigger challenge because of their mobility and ability to build up extremely rapidly. Trapping is the best method of quantifying an infestation. There are numerous types, for example sticky traps (for whitefly in glasshouses), suction traps (aphids), bait traps (slugs), and pheromone traps (pea moth, cabbage seed weevil and flour beetles in stored grain).

Disease identification presents a particular challenge. Visual diagnosis, even by experts, of, for example stem base diseases of cereals, can be unreliable and yet correct choice of control measures depend on correct identification.

Identification and evaluation

- Identify weeds when small so as to minimise herbicide dose;

- Use traps to identify and quantify insect pests;

- Diagnostic kits help the identification of some diseases but mere presence is not always a signal to spray;

- Soil analysis gives important guidance on soil-living pests;

- Walk fields regularly and be aware of pest thresholds.

A range of diagnostic kits is now available to assist in this area. However, accuracy and reliability remains a problem, and they are all qualitative rather than quantitative assessment tools. In other words, diagnosis of the presence of a disease is no indication that it will become a problem.

Other methods of identification and evaluation include soil analysis for soil living pests such as wheat bulb fly and eelworms.

Efficient pest control management cannot be carried out entirely in the laboratory or in front of the computer screen. Regular field inspection, use of competent professional advice if in doubt, and use of pest thresholds (where they are known) are all essential in the process of deciding what a pest is, and whether it needs treatment.

Pesticide choice

In many cases use of a chemical pesticide will be necessary, but the challenge for the ICM practitioner is in making the most appropriate choice. The key aspects revolve around a product's selectivity for the target pest or weed, its persistence in activity and its impact on non-target organisms.

A pesticide should always be regarded as an aid to solve a problem and its use should be integrated with other measures to minimise the problem both at the time and for the future. Most pest problems now have several chemical options available. For most people professional advice from a BASIS registered advisor is essential at this point. However, there are some basic rules to follow.

For example, where a choice of product does exist the decision will be governed by factors such as the proximity of wildlife habitats and water courses, the time of application and the nature of neighbouring crops. The chosen material must be approved for the job and, as far as possible, specific for the problem and not harmful to natural predators.

Pesticide choice

- Integrate chemical pesticides with other pest control methods;

- Do not regard chemical pesticides as a universal panacea for all problems;

- Use BASIS registered advisors;

- Always consider location, neighbouring crops, wildlife habitats and watercourses before making the choice;

- Use computerised systems as decision aids but *never* without physically inspecting the problem.

Computerised decision support systems will supposedly make the choice of product easier in future, but there is always the danger that a wealth of additional information may serve to cloud, rather than clarify, the process. In any event, pesticide choice should never be made without physically inspecting the field.

Pesticide application

Most of the difficulties that arise with the use of pesticides are normally concerned with the way they are applied.

Crop sprayers of any age are precision machines that require skill to maintain and operate efficiently. This includes regular maintenance, calibration and cleaning. Operators should be trained and most need to hold NPTC certificates of competence. Pesticide application should aim to contain a problem below a damaging threshold, rather than to eliminate it. This can be achieved by following the maxim *to use as much as necessary but as little as possible*. However it is important to remember that it is as much of a sin to underdose (thereby leaving the problem uncontrolled) as it is to overdose. In both cases chemical is introduced into the environment with no benefit.

Pesticide application

- Machinery is sophisticated: skilled and regular maintenance is essential;

- Operators must be trained with NPTC certificates if necessary;

- Aim to contain a problem rather than eliminate it;

- Use as much as necessary but as little as possible;

- Carry out COSHH assessments beforehand: prevent operator and bystander exposure;

- Observe Codes of Conduct and be especially vigilant of the weather;

- Spray accurately: avoid overlapping or missed strips;

- Be responsible about disposal of surplus, waste and the containers.

The fundamental requirement for pesticide application is accurate placement of the correct dose in the target area without allowing escape sideways or upwards by drift, or downwards by leaching and run-off. Furthermore, it must be done without contaminating users or bystanders. The Control of Substances Hazardous to Health Regulations (COSHH) are designed to control exposure to substances like pesticides by a combination of measures. They require any operator to carry out a COSHH assessment of the hazards before commencing work. Once spraying is started, following the manufacturer's instructions during use, and observing the various Codes of Conduct are all essential components of correct application. This will include keeping a careful eye on the weather, especially wind direction and strength, and ensuring accurate matching of spray swaths to avoid overlapping or missed areas. Finally it is essential to adopt responsible practices for the disposal of surplus or waste and used containers.

Keeping records

Record keeping

- Pesticide applications (date, dose, volume, timing);

- Weed mapping;

- Cropping records, including details and dates of pest problems, provide continuous farm summary;

- Maintain regular field monitoring.

It is a legal obligation to keep records of pesticide applications. In addition, however, such records provide a valuable continuous summary of pest problems on the farm. These should be supplemented by weed mapping and the normal farm cropping records. Regular field walking and simple environmental measurements can give an indication of the extent to which the overall aims of ICM are being achieved.

Conclusion

Pest control is vital in any farming system if yield, quality and profit are to be maintained. Reduction of chemical inputs is usually possible by evaluation of all available options and use of appropriate measures. The nature and size of the problem will dictate the solution, but the benefits that accrue include reduced costs, improved margins and a better safeguard for the environment.

6

Waste and
Pollution
Management

Introduction

Waste is something for which there is no practical use. Our ancestors were experts at minimising waste. They had little problem with disposing of the waste that they produced, because they had still less concern with pollution control. Combustible materials, if they could not be used on the home fire, were burnt in the open air and the smoke allowed to disperse freely. The ash would then be recycled by spreading on the land or the garden vegetable patch. Liquid wastes were simply poured away and solid materials buried.

Organic waste from the farm was recycled on the land and so, too, was human organic waste, as night-soil. Sewage disposal only became fully organised and mechanised in the middle of the nineteenth century.

The industrial revolution brought the dawn of a massive waste disposal and pollution problem. Machines running on fossil fuels produced vast, unsightly heaps of waste from the fires and furnaces, and dense black emissions into the air that subsequently deposited onto buildings and the land. From the factories came new man-made chemicals and materials for use in our clothes, in our homes and, most importantly, as packaging.

Beautiful buildings became blackened with soot, and people died from respiratory illnesses in the smog. But at the same time, knowledge of toxicology and the impact of some chemicals in everyday use, such as lead, on human health advanced rapidly. Gradually the march of progress brought with it an awareness that something had to be done. Waste disposal and pollution control thus became one of the major challenges facing modern society.

What are the particular waste disposal challenges that face agriculture?

Agriculture and horticulture have their own special problems in handling waste because many of the activities are not confined to a building or a purpose-built factory; much of it is done in the open air in areas to which the public often has free access. Furthermore, as an industry, agriculture produces significant quantities of organic waste which is not only unsightly but also often, by its very nature, smelly.

In most industrial processes, for example in factories, production and waste disposal can be managed as discrete operations. Much of the disposal of waste in agriculture and horticulture has to take place on the production site - the land. It follows that precautions need to be taken not only to protect the environment, but also to protect the soil as the fundamental natural resource for future production.

Finally, both agriculture and horticulture have responded to the challenge of meeting an increasing demand for high quality affordable food by the adoption of a wide range of new technologies. At the forefront of these are fertilisers and pesticides, both of which are potential pollutants of water and soil. Because of this, farmers and growers have a duty to adopt safe and responsible practices in managing their disposal.

Waste on the farm

Every manufacturing process – even the production of waste – consumes energy. Therefore waste products on the farm should be regarded, first and foremost, as a resource to be reused or recycled if possible, and minimised if not. Farm wastes come from a variety of sources: natural or organic waste, inorganic wastes and chemical wastes which require specialised handling because they present particular toxicological or contamination hazards.

Organic wastes include the obvious animal wastes like farm yard manure, poultry manure and slurry. Less apparent waste materials from animals are feathers, carcases and unwanted milk. Anaerobic digestion is one means of handling slurry, especially where other means of disposal might create a nitrate pollution hazard. The process produces methane which can then be used as an energy source.

Crop organic waste again includes obvious plant residues like cereal straw, sugar beet tops, and potato haulm but also materials like the green waste from packing houses, hedge trimmings and prunings.

Inorganic farm waste is derived mainly from packaging materials such as glass, metal drums, pesticide containers, plastic fertiliser bags, polythene sheeting, cardboard and paper. Also in this category one might include general litter, rubble and even stones.

Chemical wastes that require specialised handling are generally those concerned with pesticides, both concentrated and dilute, and spent sheep dip, bulb dip or fruit dip. However, also included here are washings from sprayers and pesticide containers, parlours, dairies and packing houses. Slurry and silage effluents are potent pollutants, especially of water, and are some of the most difficult wastes to handle because they are liquids and not 'contained' in the same way as pesticides, for example.

Principles of waste management

The fundamental principles of waste management are:

- *reduction* or *minimisation* of wastes with no practical value;

- *re-using* or *recycling* those wastes where suitable opportunities exist;

- *safe* and *efficient disposal* using licensed waste disposal contractors where necessary.

The plan should cover both anticipated waste disposal (crop residues, packaging etc.) and accidental waste disposal problems. Thus, contingency plans for spillages and containment of contaminated materials should all be included.

An example of how waste can be reduced is by taking steps on the farm to keep 'clean' and 'dirty' water separate. For instance, there is little point in allowing a slurry lagoon - itself a considerable investment - to be filled with rainwater when, at a little extra cost for guttering and down pipes, this water could be collected and used.

Practical steps to manage waste and pollution

Any waste that cannot be re-used or recycled is a potential pollutant, as are wastes pending their re-use. Not only is the whole farm (soil, water, air, crops and non-cropped areas) at risk, but so too is the wider environment where water and air are concerned. Therefore there is a duty of care not just within the confines of the farm, but to the community at large.

...farm waste management plan

Creation of a farm waste management plan is an essential component of an ICM system. The plan should include the identification of high pollution risk, low risk and no risk areas on the farm together with contingency plans for emergencies. To assist in this, MAFF has produced three Codes of Good Agricultural Practice covering soil, water and air. These are written as practical guides to help farmers and growers to avoid causing long-term damage to the environment in which they operate. They are not statutory documents, but in each case they describe the main causes of pollution and the risks involved. Ensuring that all staff are familiar with the guidelines offered in these Codes, as well as the farm contingency plans for emergencies, is an essential part of the forward planning for waste disposal.

...provisions for handling waste and avoiding public nuisance

Making adequate provision for handling wastes in such areas as slurry and silage storage, sheep dip handling, carcase disposal and fuel storage are obvious practical measures to take. Also included here would be systems for handling organic manure which achieve rapid incorporation or injection into the soil to ensure efficient nutrient uptake and to minimise air pollution which might otherwise antagonise neighbours. Compliance with legislation, for example in handling sewage, is obviously important.

An unfortunate, but very real, problem that many farmers face, especially those close to population centres, is fly-tipping. Under present legislation, land-owners are responsible for the disposal of dumped waste, unless the culprit can be found and convicted. Burning is the most convenient option but not always the most practical. There are strict regulations governing burning materials, especially plastics or rubber, in the open air. The creation of dense smoke is an infringement of the Clean Air Acts and any fumes or smoke can be a health risk and a safety risk if created near a public highway. The introduction, in 1996, of a new tax of £7 per tonne for waste disposed of in designated landfill sites is likely to result in an increase in fly-tipping and a consequently increased cost for farmers faced with its disposal.

Handling pesticides and fertilisers

Pesticides present special problems because of statutory constraints concerning their use, the disposal of their containers and their presence in water and produce. The EC Drinking Water Directive imposes maximum admissible concentrations for all pesticides (irrespective of their toxicity) and nitrogen and it is therefore important to avoid contaminating surface or groundwaters with these chemicals. Furthermore their presence on the wrong crop, or in hedge-rows and other non-target areas are forms of pollution. Finally, gross contamination of land can place severe constraints on what may be grown subsequently.

For all these reasons, pesticides and fertilisers require specialised management from the moment they arrive on the farm to the time when any surplus material, together with the containers, are disposed of. Various steps can be taken long before they are actually applied in the field. Accurate application of these materials in the field contributes a lot to the minimisation of waste and therefore risk.

...storage

It is inevitable that, for a lot of the time, some pesticides have to be stored on the farm. They are not only valuable - theft is not uncommon - but they are potentially hazardous to users, other people and the environment. Storage of pesticides places heavy responsibilities on everyone concerned who must take all reasonable precautions to protect the health of human beings, creatures and plants, and to safeguard the environment. Avoiding the pollution of water, whether in day-to-day management or following accident or spillage, is of particular importance.

In general, chemical stores must meet specified minimum standards in such matters as security, fire resistance, weather proofing and containment of spillages and leakage. Detailed guidance on the legal requirements of pesticide storage, together with information about the construction and siting of pesticide stores is available from the Health and Safety Executive.

... getting ready to use pesticides

Accurate application makes sense from both economic and environmental viewpoints. Underdosing or overdosing, or merely failing to ensure even application across the delivery width of the machine, are inefficient uses of these chemicals. At the very least these mistakes make the crop look unsightly, while more often damage to the crop or failure to control the pest reduce its yield or its quality. Yet, in spite of this, over half of all pesticide sprayers in UK are never calibrated, and a similar proportion of fertiliser spreader operators have never read the machine manual. Providing training for operators and, where appropriate, ensuring that they have the necessary Certificate of Competence, is the vital first step. This needs to be followed up by checking that the lessons learnt are actually applied in practice.

...turning the legal approval into practical safety

In UK, government approval of a pesticide is obligatory before it may be sold or used. Approval is an assurance that the product can achieve effective pest control without unacceptable risk to humans or the environment, provided it is used correctly. The product label stipulates legally binding limitations about how it should be used. The crops that may be sprayed, the maximum dose that should be applied and the interval that should elapse before harvest are all listed.

Once in the field, the onus clearly rests with the operator. In-field checks of spillages, spray or spread patterns, together with an awareness of the need to protect watercourses and hedgerows, are all practical measures to ensure that the safety indicated by the product approval is achieved in practice. Accurate records must be kept.

...disposing of the surplus

Mixing only as much as you need is a prerequisite for efficient pesticide use. Nevertheless some surplus dilute pesticide is unavoidable and its disposal is a challenge that requires careful management. It is certainly not good practice to leave it in the sprayer. The legally binding conditions of the pesticide approval will normally prevent disposal of any surplus in the sprayer onto another, different, crop. Even using it up on the crop just treated is not possible unless it (or a part of it) has been deliberately underdosed. The same constraints apply to any contaminated water resulting from washing out the sprayer or pesticide containers. Here again there are guidelines in the Code of Practice and forward planning can help to minimise the scale of the problem in the first place, by careful calculation of the amount needed for the job.

...disposing of plastic containers, bags and sheeting

The pesticide containers themselves will often have guidance for safe disposal on the label. Where this is not the case, the normal correct procedure is to rinse three times followed by burial, or burning where this is permitted. Plastic sheeting and fertiliser bags are also often burned, but there should be few circumstances where other practical methods of disposal cannot be found. Ideally materials should be burned only if there is no other practical method of disposal and then they should be handled in an incinerator rather than in the open. Where an incinerator is used, the installation may require authorisation by the local authority under Part I of the Environmental Protection Act 1990.

Recycling plastic materials

Suitable polythene materials for recycling include:

* Silage bags and sheets;

* Polythene inners from fertiliser 'big bags';

* 50 kg fertiliser bags;

* Pallet covers;

* Polythene covers from greenhouses.

Apart from pesticide containers, many plastic materials can be reused or recycled, and the possibilities for this should always be addressed in the farm waste disposal plan. If an item can be used several times before it becomes unserviceable, the volume of plastic for disposal is greatly reduced. If re-use or recycling is not practicable then biodegradable plastic materials should be chosen wherever possible. Guidance on the re-use and recycling of plastics, as well as the disposal of those items for which there is no alternative, is given in the MAFF *Code of Good Agricultural Practice for the Protection of Air*. This is an area of rapidly changing legislation and awareness of any changes is part of managing an ICM system.

...bulk supply and returnable containers

Some fertilisers are already delivered in bulk thereby reducing the amount of packaging involved but possibly increasing storage difficulties. Storage areas should be on level, well-drained ground without projections or snags which could cause puncturing or tearing of packages. Ideally they should be sited away from population centres, but if this is unavoidable, the bulk storage should be surveyed frequently if there is a risk of vandalism.

The pesticide industry is taking the first steps towards the supply of chemicals in returnable containers, with some suppliers setting voluntary targets for the reduction of plastic waste by the end of the century. This is in response to a European Directive that requires 58% of all pesticide packaging to be recovered by the year 2001, of which 25% must be recycled for other uses such as fence posts. Already farmers in Belgium and Austria have to pay for the disposal of empty chemical containers.

Returnable containers bring the added benefit of closed filling systems, in which the chances of spillage and operator or environmental contamination during filling and rinsing are dramatically reduced. In the meantime the industry is playing an important part in helping to alleviate the problems by formulating pesticides as effervescent tablets or water soluble granules. These can be packaged in water-soluble sachets where users can safely burn the outer cardboard packaging in areas where this is permitted. Increasing the concentration of the pesticide itself also reduces the amount of packaging required.

...unused pesticide

Unused pesticide concentrate should be kept in the original container, tightly closed in a safe place - under lock and key if the label so directs. It might be possible to dispose of unopened containers to a neighbour, or even back to the original supplier. If not, it will be necessary to use a reputable licensed waste disposal contractor who will also handle opened containers if there is no foreseeable use on the farm. It is not good practice to keep opened pesticide containers for any length of time, and those that are kept must be sound and securely closed with the original label firmly attached.

The benefits of managing farm waste

A farm waste management policy demands attention to detail and ensures better use of resources. The result is a more profitable business. To this is added the benefit of a reduced risk of prosecution and consequent heavy fines for pollution. There are also benefits in public relations terms. A well-managed farm that is kept tidy and clear of litter, rusting pesticide containers and plastic fertiliser bags is a visible and reassuring sign to the public of an efficient and conscientiously run business. Obviously they will need the same reassurance in other aspects, such as quality of produce, but much of that stems from proper controls of waste and pollution in the first place.

Finally, the employees themselves have the assurance of working in an environment that not only seeks to minimise pollution of soil, water and air, but also has clear emergency procedures and an emergency action plan to cater for unforseen circumstances.

Conclusion

Careless waste disposal procedures are potentially damaging to the environment, to the public perception about farming and to the economy of the business. A carefully written farm waste management plan is an essential component of an ICM system.

7

Energy
Management

Introduction

Energy costs money, but it is an invisible resource and therefore easy to waste. Furthermore, without meticulous records, it is difficult to assign the quarterly fuel bill to different parts of a business. Most energy is generated from fossil fuels which are themselves a finite resource and which increase the burden of atmospheric carbon dioxide when they are burnt. So, on both economic and environmental grounds, it makes sense to make the best use of energy on the farm. This means increasing the efficiency of energy use, and eliminating waste.

The three most commonly used fuels on a farm are fossil fuel, gas and electricity to meet energy requirements in the form of heat, light and power. However, it should not be forgotten that fertilisers (especially nitrogen) and, to a lesser extent, pesticides represent significant but essential inputs of energy in addition to the one major natural source – sunlight. Fertilisers and pesticides are discussed in other chapters. Here we are concerned with the use of fossil fuels.

The main energy consuming functions on any farm are:

- Powering farm vehicles and field machinery such as combine harvesters, balers, sugar beet harvesters;

- Powering static machinery such as driers, ventilators, grain elevators, milking equipment, pumps;

- Lighting the farm buildings, livestock houses, glasshouses, offices and any domestic premises;

- Heating (or cooling) in livestock houses, cold stores, refrigeration units, offices and domestic premises.

Practical steps to reduce consumption

Most people are conscious of the need to turn off lights and shut doors in the home to conserve energy. Similarly, driving a car well within its performance capability without undue use of accelerator and brake is a technique likely to improve fuel economy and prolong the life of the vehicle. Integrated Crop

Management requires that the same principles are applied to the whole farm business in a more structured and formalised manner.

Part of this process might be, for example, the substitution of one type of machinery with another. A good example is the handling and treatment of liquid animal waste, which can be a big problem on the farm. Electric pumps are easily installed, can be remotely controlled and can utilise cheaper night rate electricity. In this way tractor power can be released for other work. In the field, careful management of fertiliser and pesticide use, the use of flotation tyres and tracks, and careful adjustment of tyre pressures are all energy-saving measures.

Sensible judgements about managing energy can only be made with a detailed analysis of current practice. A farm energy audit which sets down all costs and energy consumption is the only way to start. Even if the audit reveals that some important records are not kept, it will have served a valuable purpose! After that, the various activities can be studied in more detail and a farm energy plan formulated.

...vehicles and machinery

Economy starts at the time of purchase; fuel consumption should be a major consideration. The tractors on the farm should be capable of meeting predicted needs. This requires careful assessment of the overall demand for power so that horsepower can be matched to need. All farm vehicles and machinery should be regularly serviced and this should include fuel consumption and emission measurements, as well as adjustment of tyre pressures for maximum efficiency of operation.

Paradoxically, having obtained the equipment, the aim should be to minimise its use. An obvious, but often overlooked, waste is vehicle idling. Clearly a balance has to be struck between frequent restarting and leaving machines running, but extended idling is not good for the machine itself. Field operations, such as cultivation and drilling, or drilling and rolling, should be combined wherever possible so that the number of passes over the land are minimised. This has to be balanced against the additional power that might be needed and the consequent extra damage to soil structure.

Haulage distances and general vehicle movements can often be reduced by spending some time planning ahead. This can be helped by measures such as providing an in-field water supply when spraying, and the use of radio or telephone to improve communications between staff on the farm.

Careful record keeping is the only way to manage fuel consumption. Consumption figures should be kept for each vehicle and machine so that the overall cost can be correctly apportioned. This will then give an indication of comparative performance and efficiency which will become a guideline at the time of the next purchase.

Static machinery

Many of the same considerations are relevant, but the principle of 'out of sight, out of mind' can easily apply to a machine like a pump or a drier that is left to run, perhaps for 24 hours a day. So long as it *sounds* alright the temptation is to assume that it is alright. Static machines need to be maintained on a regular basis, and their fuel consumption and emissions monitored. The possibility of updating and modernising equipment should be constantly reviewed in the context of improved efficiency.

Other steps to consider are the installation of remote or automatic control equipment such as time switches and thermostats. In the case of electrical equipment, control equipment to take advantage of low cost tariffs is another possibility.

...grain storage

Grain needs to be stored on the farm whether for the purpose of orderly marketing or for keeping for livestock feed. The process requires control of the moisture content and temperature so that organisms that cause deterioration cannot develop. Where the incoming grain is at too high a moisture content, it must be dried at the beginning of the storage period. The process is expensive in terms of energy consumption, especially where continuous flow or other high temperature driers are used to evaporate the surplus moisture rapidly. However on most farms the major component in drying costs is the overhead cost of the equipment itself. Any cost-saving plan should address this aspect first before considering energy consumption. However, if the grain is to kept on the farm after drying, energy costs can be reduced by combining the functions of drying and storage. Of course, major savings can be made by timely harvesting of a clean crop which requires no drying prior to storage.

...vegetable storage

Conditioning and storage of fresh vegetable produce to meet a market demand that is far wider than the normal harvest 'window' is a precision task. In most cases it is necessary to create a gradual steady temperature drop in the store from the 'field' temperature to the optimum storage temperature. Often this is close to $0°C$, but it is also necessary to prevent any frost damage if temperatures fall lower than this. Although manual control of ventilation can be used, it entails a considerable degree of management and supervision. This can be replaced by the use of a differential electrical thermostat with probes in the produce and in the outside atmosphere. Almost certainly this will represent a more efficient use of electrical energy as well as significantly reducing the risk of storage losses.

Lighting and heating

Any requirement for lighting for safety or security should not be compromised. However, the use of time switches, movement sensing switches and energy efficient bulbs (eg fluorescent tubes) are all worth considering. Heating equipment, especially oil-fired boilers, can become inefficient with age, even with regular servicing. At the time of updating or modernising, simultaneous consideration can be given to switching fuel, from oil to gas for example.

The term 'environmental control' in agriculture refers to the balancing of temperature by ventilation and heating. It is mainly used in controlling the climate in livestock housing, but it can also refer to controlling the environment in crop and produce stores. In the latter case it may also include adjustment of carbon dioxide, oxygen or nitrogen levels. The extent of energy input required will nearly always be determined by the insulation in the fabric of the building.

Most householders know that the biggest single reason for loss of heat from the home is poor insulation in the roof, the walls and the windows. The same applies to farm buildings. Improving the insulation of existing buildings can be difficult if they are very old but energy conservation should have high priority in the planning of any new buildings.

Alternatives

As technology advances, the possibility of using alternative sources of energy should be continually reviewed. Solar energy and wind can be harnessed, although often at some environmental cost. Some crop residues, for example straw, prunings and forestry waste are sources of energy, albeit limited. Growing willow or poplar biomass or bio-diesel from rape oil are all future possible alternatives to the use of fossil fuels.

The recently published *National Biomass Strategy* from the UK Government outlines a five-year plan for encouraging the development of renewable energy production from crops such as short rotation coppice and agricultural by-products such as straw, poultry litter and slurry.

Conclusion

As with everything else in ICM, energy consumption and utilisation can only be managed if it is measured. Investment of one or two hours on a farm energy audit together with regular monitoring and meticulous record-keeping are the ways forward. Existing practices can be assessed and future improvements planned. The audit provides the baseline against which progress can be measured.

Inefficient use of non-renewable fossil energy is costly and wasteful in any business. To be compatible with the principles of ICM, energy consumption needs to be monitored and optimised.

Wildlife and Landscape Management

Introduction

...factories and farms

Work places can be ugly, dedicated to their purpose, often noisy and sometimes dirty. Raw materials are taken in at one end of, say, a factory, and the finished product emerges at the other. The processes that take place in between are strictly controlled and largely unseen. There will be significant measures to ensure the safety of the people who work there but, beyond that, the place will be functional rather than beautiful. Access will nearly always be restricted to authorised personnel who, at the end of their work, are able to turn their backs and go home. Certainly there is no place for the unwanted visitor and squatters will be forcibly ejected. Not so for the farmer.

The farmer's production site is the land: visible to all, often publicly accessible, and home for a wide range of plants and animals, not just the ones he wants, or is trying to grow. It is also his home and, by universal acclaim, naturally beautiful although few, if challenged, could articulate a definition of what this means. It is a dynamic living environment in which the farmer harnesses the natural resources of energy and nutrients to grow his crops and animals. It is a factory where it is not sufficient merely to adopt safe practices, although this is essential. It is a factory where many plant and animal visitors are welcome and where even the forcible ejection of squatters – the pests – is regarded by many as undesirable. Most important, it is a factory whose product is needed by everyone.

Has technology taken over?

Because of the fundamental requirement to provide food for a rapidly growing population, farming has intensified in the second half of the twentieth century. The emphasis has been on production, with a steady increase in inputs to the point where, to many people, farming is now over-reliant on technology. Phrases like 'factory farming' for some aspects of livestock production, have entered the vocabulary. In truth, the reverse is the case.

In spite of the benefits of modern technology, without the natural processes of the utilisation of sunlight energy, the fixation of atmospheric nitrogen, the creation by earthworms of soil crumb-structure, the microbial breakdown of organic residues and much, much more, the efforts of man would be worthless.

Farming is the process of harnessing the natural resources and sometimes modifying them to produce food.

Nevertheless, in the process of intensification the focus on output has sometimes neglected the other aspects of the land that make up the elusive quality of beauty. Some of the basic values and skills, built up over generations of farming tradition, have been overlooked. The march of agricultural progress has stripped the landscape of many hedgerows and trees, ponds and water meadows, all of which play host to a rich diversity of wildlife. With the supply of their food assured, the public demand is for farmers to be more sensitive to the issues of wildlife and environmental protection.

ICM seeks to redress the balance

Integrated farm management sets out to find ways that enable a commercially viable business to run at the same time as ensuring that the countryside remains attractive and richly stocked with wildlife. Such a move towards more environmentally conscious farming means that there are many options to be considered and sometimes difficult decisions to make.

A carefully considered plan of action is essential and it must embrace the whole farm. The basis of this is an appraisal of the farm as an operating unit and assistance in doing this is obtainable from specialist agencies such as Farming and Wildlife Groups (FWAG) or ADAS. FWAG is based at the National Agricultural Centre at Stoneleigh, Coventry, Warwickshire (Telephone: 01203 696699); ADAS is based at Oxford Spires Business Park, The Boulevard, Kidlington, Oxford (Telephone: 01865 842742).

Every bit of land counts, commercially and environmentally, but here, as with all aspects of ICM, there are no prescriptive rules on what should, or should not, be done. Much of the secret of success lies in awareness, not just by the manager but by everyone who works there, of the habits, needs and benefits of wildlife on the farm.

Assess the wildlife and habitat features of the farm

In this area of farm management, more than any other, the decisions often depend on value judgements rather than hard facts, and the options may conflict. Nevertheless, the process starts with a factual survey of the wildlife habitats and landscape features of the farm. A large scale map can be created to show all watercourses, ponds, lakes and other wet areas, trees and woodland and other non-cropped areas, including set-aside. It should also show the nature of all field margins and boundaries, whether hedges, walls, fences, tracks or grass strips. Any footpaths and bridleways, together with the position and function of buildings and monuments should all be shown.

Practical steps

The practical steps to be taken will vary from farm to farm, but the same underlying principles apply in most cases. It is no excuse to claim that a particular piece of land or a farm is not environmentally sensitive, or does not display any features of outstanding natural beauty. Every farmer is able to do something, however small, to protect and enhance the environment. The main emphasis should be placed on conserving and managing the existing features. New features to enhance the landscape and conservation value of the farm should be introduced but not at the expense of valuable existing habitats. There is no shortage of information or help; the main problem facing the farmer is how to distil the information into a coherent action plan.

MAFF have recently produced guidelines, in a joint project with RSPB, to help farmers become more aware of what they can do to protect birds whose numbers have fallen significantly over the past 20 years. Farmers can often significantly improve conditions for these species by making relatively small changes in their farming practice. The guidelines describe the practical measures farmers can take.

...cropped and uncropped areas

In both cropped and uncropped areas, field margins and headlands are important conservation areas. Where possible an uncultivated strip along any field boundary should be left and misapplication or drift of fertilisers and pesticides onto uncultivated land should be avoided. Autumn stubbles are sources of seeds and invertebrates for mammals during the winter while spring crops, set-aside and fallow provide nesting sites for birds.

MAFF/RSPB farmland bird recovery project

Designed to raise awareness amongst farmers, advisors and students of the importance of environmentally sensitive farm management for the conservation of farmland birds. The guidelines cover seven species for which studies by the British Trust for Ornithology have shown population declines on farmland.

Species	Population decline 1968–91
Grey Partridge	-73%
Lapwing	-47%
Skylark	-54%
Reed Bunting	-59%
Linnet	-56%
Corn Bunting	-76%
Tree Sparrow	-85%

Source: British Trust for Ornithology

Set-aside, much maligned for other reasons, can have a positive influence on farm wildlife, and has proved to be less troublesome than once feared as farmers have learned how to manage it and benefit from it. A recent two-year study by the Royal Society for the Protection of Birds has shown that set-aside fields have significantly increased numbers of skylarks, goldfinches, greenfinches, linnets and yellowhammers compared with cropped fields.

Excessive cultivations damage soil structure and many operations are a threat to wildlife. Rolling, spraying and cutting in the spring months can destroy nests as well as young, and even adult, birds. Ploughing permanent grassland should be avoided if possible. If this is impractical, it should be ploughed in spring and reseeded as quickly as possible to ensure capture of the massive release of nutrients. When harvesting cereals or cutting grass for hay or silage, wildlife can escape if the field is handled in sections rather than working towards the centre from the edges.

Recently, further changes to the set-aside management rules have been made by MAFF with the aim of improving the environmental benefits without imposing unreasonable costs on farmers. The most significant benefit for ground nesting birds is an increase from 10% to 25% of the area of any set-aside field that can be left uncut in any year in order to provide a more varied habitat. The area can now be left uncut for up to three years.

Changes to set-aside management rules

- A ban on cutting and cultivation between 1 April and 15 July;

- Increase of the area that may be left uncut and the period it may remain uncut;

- Reduction of the minimum qualifying strip width.

...pesticides and fertilisers

Pesticides and fertilisers require careful handling. Treatments should always be carefully targeted and matched to calculated requirements. Nitrogen, by encouraging luxuriant growth of the most vigorous plant species, reduces the diversity of natural communities of plants. Applications in the later part of the year should be avoided where possible to reduce leaching into underground water reserves. Avoid applying fertilisers onto uncultivated field margins or into the bottom of hedgerows and take particular care with liquid manures and slurry. Ideally, they should be injected or applied through low-level booms. Application on frozen ground should be avoided.

Pesticides should be used on the basis of as little as possible but as much as necessary, and particular care is needed along hedgerows or near water. Some products have specific restrictions about spraying near watercourses, and these should always be followed. Even where no such warning is given, consideration should be given to leaving a buffer zone if it can be seen that there is a risk of spoiling a wildlife haven. This does not mean that treatment would necessarily kill the creatures that live there, but if it is a herbicide, it might easily destroy the habitat. Local bee-keepers should be warned of impending operations that might endanger their hives. Slugs can be reduced by paying attention to the quality of the seedbed, but where control is needed, the pellets should be drilled with the crop and covered, rather than broadcast on the soil surface.

...water

Water is an important natural resource for many farmers but it is also one of the most vulnerable parts of the farm environment. Watercourses and ditches channel away surface and drainage water from fields. But, in addition to its aesthetic and amenity value, water is also an important factor in enriching the diversity of wildlife on the farm.

As well as mapping all the water features, the starting point is to note its condition in terms of acidity and the plant and invertebrate life it supports. The plan should aim to integrate 'wildlife havens' into the management of watercourses. This can be achieved by, for example, cleaning ditches on alternate sides in alternate years, and carrying out ditch management tasks in the autumn. Short untrimmed lengths of vegetation can be left along the banks.

Wet areas in field corners, instead of being regarded as productively 'dead', can be seen as an opportunity to create a lake or a pond without significant loss to the field output. Vegetation growing in ponds might be the result of high nitrate levels but, in any event, it will need to be contained and ideally this should be done mechanically rather than chemically. Other pollutants, such as silage liquor or slurry, must be rigorously avoided. Ponds should not be excessively shaded by trees and livestock access should be limited.

...trees and woodland

Trees take a long time to grow, but can be quickly destroyed. It is important to establish a long-term woodland management plan for the farm, with particular attention to the management of any ancient woodland. Open space within woodland, and even standing dead timber, are valuable habitats for many forms of wildlife. Once again, the first step is to make a survey of the existing woodland noting such things as species, their age and condition, and the presence of woodland animals and insects. Special requirements and uses need to be identified at this stage. These might include livestock shelters, shooting cover, and screens for buildings, or there might be commercial uses such as forestry or Norway Spruce. Opportunities to establish new areas of woodland should be sought with the aim of creating a balanced mixture of young, middle-aged and older trees on the farm.

...field margins, hedges and walls

Fences and hedges

- In UK there are   421,000 miles of fences;
  300,000 miles of hedges.

- In ten years since 1983: hedges have reduced by 20%;
  diversity has reduced by 7%.

Source: Barr et al. RASE Journal 1994 pp 48–58

Hedgerows and field margins are havens for birds and beneficial species like spiders and beetles, but they also harbour weeds, insect pests and diseases. Here conservation means finding a balance between the measures necessary to contain the pests and those required to encourage other beneficial or non-target species. A hedge management plan will schedule all hedges on the farm to be trimmed every 2–3 years, although it is useful to leave hedges uncut in places, particularly at hedge junctions. The aim should be to manage a variety of hedge types on the farm in terms of size, shape and composition. Any operations should be avoided during nesting time and ideally should be delayed until late in the winter so the supply of seeds and berries is not destroyed. In fields containing stock, the hedge can be protected from damage by using an inner wire fence. Overgrown hedges should be coppiced and new growth trimmed or laid. If pernicious weeds are present and threaten to invade the field edge, it is best to use a herbicide that is as specific as possible to the problem. The impact of any control measures should be carefully monitored.

...conservation headlands and beetle banks

Naturally occurring predatory arthropods are a great help to the farmer in keeping some pests, for example aphids, at levels below a damaging threshold. Many of these beneficial species live and overwinter in the hedgerows or the ground. The greatest threat to these species lies in a farming system that seeks to maximise land use, and minimise the amount of unproductive ground. Larger fields and use of heavier and more powerful machinery are manifestations of this, and the result is that the natural vegetation of the field margin is greatly reduced.

The Game Conservancy Trust have evolved a series of guidelines for the management of headlands designed to reverse this trend while at the same time avoiding significant penalties on agricultural production. The management technique involves the selective reduction of the use of pesticides on the outer 6 m of the crop to create a "Conservation Headland". Although they were originally developed with the specific aim of protecting game birds, especially the grey partridge, conservation headlands are demonstrably helpful for the survival of many other non-target species.

Clearly, if fields are very large, the amount of natural pest protection in the centre is reduced because of the limited ability of many predatory arthropods to travel great distances. Where fields are much larger than 16 ha (40 acres) the process can be assisted by providing havens for these species by planting grassy strips across the field. These 'beetle banks' provide shelter and refuge, as well as food, to assist population build-up of the predators which can then readily access the crop when pest attack occurs. Professional advice on the establishment and management of beetle banks is also available from The Game Conservancy Trust.

Landscape and amenity features

Footpaths and bridleways quickly deteriorate unless they are properly managed. This is an important element of Integrated Crop Management since it is one the most effective ways of demonstrating care for the amenity value of the landscape to the outside world. The paths themselves should be kept clear of overhanging vegetation and signposts and stiles need to be inspected regularly and repaired if necessary. Ploughing or cultivating headland footpaths or bridleways is illegal.

Grants and other support may well be available for the creation of new amenity features on the farm, such as nature trails. Grant aid is available from a variety of source for a wide range of ventures such as habitat improvement, the protection of field monuments and historic buildings and countryside access. Details of these schemes can be obtained from FWAG, ADAS, local authorities, the Scottish Agricultural College or the Department of Agriculture for Northern Ireland.

Farm grants for care of the environment

There are many schemes available aimed at promoting care for the environment, wildlife or historic buildings, and improving the amenity value on the farm. The schemes are continually changing and up-to-date advice should be sought from the relevant body. Examples are:

- The Woodland Grant Scheme;

- The Farm Woodland Premium Scheme;

- The Farm and Conservation Grant Scheme;

- Grants for the protection of field monuments and historic buildings;

- The Habitat Improvement Scheme

- The Country Stewardship Scheme;

- The Countryside Access Scheme.

Conclusion

Progress can only be demonstrated to others if it is monitored and measured. Mapping the farm wildlife havens and regular simple monitoring, keeping accurate records of indicator species of birds, mammals and plant life provide the yardsticks of progress. They are an essential part of an Integrated Crop Management system.

Environmental performance evaluation needs to set objective measurable criteria against which actual performance can be judged. The objectives are set down in the farm landscape and wildlife plan so that conservation becomes an integral part of running the business. The emphasis must be on active management and understanding of the problems. Achievement needs to be monitored so that it can be shown that environmental protection can coexist with profitable farming. It is a global issue in which all farmers and landowners have a part to play. For many, all that is required is a change of attitude, from viewing environmental improvement as a luxury to be indulged where there is time and money to spare, to routinely combining conservation and farming activities. Many of the necessary actions cost nothing, and some will even save money.

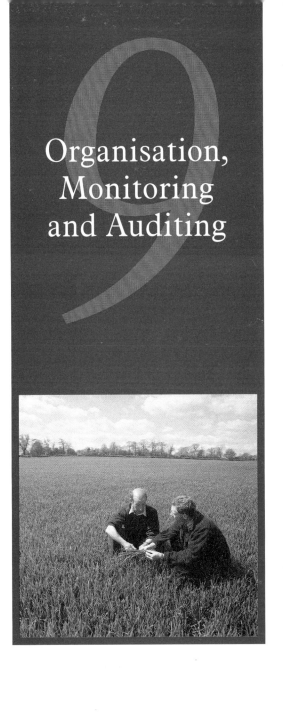

Organisation, Monitoring and Auditing

Introduction

Any successful business needs an organised and structured framework in which to operate. People must have a clear idea of what they are expected to do and they need to see this in the context of what the business is trying to achieve as a whole. Individual performance is likely to be better if the business objectives are explained so that they can see how their individual effort contributes to the overall achievement. The business itself must set realistic targets and progress towards achieving them needs to be measured. Above all, any business must be flexible and adapt to changing circumstances. New technologies, or changing customer requirements, must be continually monitored and the business plan modified where necessary.

...accountability and integrity

The result is that not only does the business thrive, but, by looking at the records, it can see where mistakes were made. This experience can be used to improve future efficiency. Above all, the business is fully accountable, whether to directors, partners or customers. If the records have been kept, people can make their own judgments about the overall business integrity.

Integrated Crop Management requires all this.

Farming is a business more vulnerable than most to the vagaries of climate and customer choice. It is an industry where remarkable technological advances have been made over the past 50 years, and farmers and growers are no strangers to adaptability and change. For most of them, the adoption of Integrated Crop Management practices is a case of fine tuning, and adopting a systematic approach, rather wholesale change. But for some the discipline of setting targets, monitoring progress and constantly auditing performance may be new.

What needs to be done?

...time

Like any management policy, Integrated Crop Management requires an investment of time and commitment to make it work. Time is a valuable resource that requires personal time management as well as appropriate delegation of work, setting priorities and checking progress. This involves planning, and throughout this booklet there has been emphasis on creation of plans in all the main activities as well as contingency planning for emergencies. Awareness of these measures would form part of a staff development and training plan in which all requirements are identified and achievements monitored. The staff themselves should contribute to the creation of all the farm plans.

...targets

Setting targets is more difficult, but the golden rule must be to make sure they are realistic and measurable. The first action in the implementation of an Integrated Crop Management system is the creation of a written farm policy setting out the aims and objectives. Areas that might be included are financial targets for the business, crop performance targets (yield and quality), fuel consumption, nitrogen use, water quality. The keeping of full and accurate records is itself an achievement target.

Targets in Integrated Crop Management

Setting achievement targets is analogous to putting milestones on the road. They are the measure of progress and the record of success. They might include:

- Environmental tasks e.g hedge planting;
- Financial (i.e. profit) targets;
- Crop performance (yield and quality);
- Fuel consumption;
- Water quality;
- Staff training;
- Farm performance (e.g. in competitions).

...information and advice

Technological advances in farming have meant that nobody can hope to keep abreast of it all. Information or professional advice is certain to be needed from time to time and this is a crucial part of the decision making process. The first step is to decide what information and advice is needed. Ideally professional advisers should be independent, although the quality of the advice given is the important thing. Fertiliser or pesticide advisors should be FACTS or BASIS qualified respectively. Other means of keeping up-to-date are by reading journals and literature, using information services, including the Internet, and attending conferences, demonstrations (including LEAF demonstration farms) and shows.

...communication

Effective communication plays an important part in business. Staff need to be kept informed about the overall business as well as the day to day tasks. Understanding the reasons for the farm policies and actions is an important part of gaining staff commitment to the system. Similarly management needs to hear, and respond to, staff suggestions or complaints. Externally it is important to remember that 'customers' extend far beyond those with whom direct business is done. By its very nature, farming embraces whole communities and, eventually, the general public as consumers.

The essence of integrated farm management is not just the adoption of environmentally responsible practices. It includes the communication of the benefits to a public that harbours, with justification in some cases, scepticism about modern methods. The best way is to invite them to see and hear what is being done. This is done by liaison with the local community through meetings and farm visits, and by hosting external demonstrations. Customers should not be excluded from the process. They all have businesses to run and a reciprocal appreciation of needs and policies avoids misunderstandings and improves relationships.

Monitoring

Monitoring is the regular checking of measurable objectives and targets, such as fuel consumption or fertiliser use. The information gained provides a series of markers against which performance can be plotted. Subjective judgements of things like the amenity value of a woodland, although important, are imprecise management tools because they are unquantifiable. Management requires measurement.

In many ways routine monitoring is a means of updating the information gathered in the initial site survey. The structure of the soil, the condition of hedges, fences and walls and the state of ponds and waterways all form part of routine day to day observations.

...crops and pests

Whatever management system is practised, growing crops should be inspected regularly to check vigour and growth stages, and to note the appearance of any pest problems. This should be more frequent as the time for treatment approaches, or after weather conditions known to favour the spread of a particular problem. Infestations should be counted or assessed and compared with treatment thresholds to help in decisions about control measures.

Pest incidence, especially the precise location of some weed infestations, such as wild oats, should be carefully recorded and mapped for use in future seasons. Similarly, any pest carry-over from previous crops, or spread from neighbouring fields and farms, should be noted. Wherever possible, pest incidence should be quantified by use of traps, baits, diagnostic kits or simple weed counts and matched against any known thresholds.

...soil, wildlife and landscape

Crop walking should include routine soil checks on moisture content, erosion and compaction. Regular soil and leaf tissue analyses help with the calculation of fertiliser requirements, and actual fertiliser use should be monitored. For each field a nutrient balance sheet should be kept quantifying nutrient inputs and offtake and so allowing calculation of field surpluses or deficits.

Cultivation machinery maintenance should be checked regularly and records kept of all cultivations carried out, including a note of any problem areas. Simple monitoring of selected wildlife indicator species gives a measure of the impact of other farm practices and helps to show the effect of any changes made to the management system. Crop inspections can be coupled with checks on hedgerows, field margins and nesting sites in stubbles and set-aside.

The state of footpaths and bridleways, stiles and gates, and signposts should also form part of the routine monitoring. Footpaths in particular, after a wet winter and during the onset of spring growth, may well need attention. Good relationships with the local community are not fostered by leaving footpaths in an unwalkable condition. For their part, walkers may seek alternative routes which can result in damage to fences and hedges, and even to crops.

...energy, waste and pollution

Monitoring gross fuel consumption is relatively simple, although the allocation of the costs to individual pieces of equipment requires more detailed record keeping. Regular servicing of vehicles can lead to savings in petrol and diesel fuel. The state of any insulation can have a significant effect on the use (or waste) of heat. Records should be kept and monitored. Fertiliser spreaders and pesticide sprayers should be routinely calibrated and in-field performance regularly checked by operators. Necessary repairs should be carried out promptly.

Whilst some waste is inevitable it should be minimised. Achievement of the targets set in the farm waste management plan should be monitored to see that the guidance in the Codes of Good Agricultural Practice is being followed. Disposal of surplus pesticide and used pesticide containers requires specialist treatment. Where this involves burning (together with other plastics) emissions of smoke must be carefully controlled. Other pollutants, such as effluents, smells and even noise, must be monitored and checks made to ensure that reduction measures are working effectively.

Water quality must always be watched carefully. Unlike most features on the farm, water is not self-contained. It passes through and may be used elsewhere for a variety of purposes, one of which might be the supply of drinking water. Agriculture produces a variety of potential water pollutants: these include silage effluent, slurry and other organic waste, fertilisers and pesticides. Management to protect water quality starts with a general survey of its existing condition from which a long term management plan can be formed. Where fertilisers and pesticides are concerned this involves careful evaluation of storage, transport, use and disposal.

The water quality itself should be monitored by observation of the wildlife living in and around it. This will include a range of water-living insects and snails, together with floating and emergent plants. Guidance on the indicator species to look for can be obtained from the local Farming and Wildlife Advisory Group (FWAG) Advisor.

Finally, routine checks should be made to ensure that staff are aware of the farm procedures for handling emergencies.

Auditing

Audit definition

A management tool comprising a systematic, documented, periodic and objective evaluation of performance.

Routine monitoring gathers information about what is happening on the farm. Auditing is the process of using this information to review achievement against the agreed targets and standards that have been built into the overall ICM plan for the farm.

Ideally a farm audit should be carried out annually, and the LEAF Environmental Audit is a ready made management tool designed for this purpose. Essentially it is a critical self-analysis of the impact of the farming practice on the surroundings. It answers the question 'what are we doing now?' and poses the questions 'what do we want to achieve?' and 'what do we need to change?'. This helps the decisions about what improvements or changes, if any, are necessary.

Total package traceability

As well as evaluation of existing practices and identification of areas for improvement, auditing carries a number of long-term benefits:

- Improving economic performance;
- Enhancing environmental protection;
- Meeting insurance requirements;
- Meeting legislative requirements;
- Gaining commercial advantage;
- Addressing public concerns;
- Financial planning and control.

Integrated Crop Management seeks to ensure the economic, but profitable, production of crops by using methods that conserve and enhance the environment. An audit provides a quantitative measure with which to demonstrate that this is being achieved. There are a number of benefits that arise from this. Internally, it helps in the achievement of targets and greatly facilitates the management of environmental protection. Externally it indicates a quality standard and provides information about the business for insurers and bankers. Most of all, it provides reassurance for customers and the public that the business is carried out not only responsibly and professionally but also sensitively.

Conclusion

There are no absolute measures of what constitutes good performance in an Integrated Crop Management system. Every farm or holding has to draw up its own plans and set its own targets in which every decision has been considered and justified both economically and environmentally. Auditing progress against these targets is an essential part of management and helps to determine priorities for action. Setting standards and targets provides a means by which the benefits of ICM can be quantified and demonstrated. The process requires leadership, input of management time and commitment from everyone concerned.

Sources of Information

For further information contact:

ATB-Landbase
National Agricultural Centre,
Kenilworth, Warwickshire CV8 2LG
Tel: 01203 696996 Fax: 01203 696732

ADAS
Oxford Spires Business Park,
The Boulevard, Kidlington,
Oxfordshire OX5 1NZ
Tel: 01865 845033 Fax: 01865 845055

BASIS
BASIS (Registration) Ltd,
2 St John Street, Ashbourne,
Derbyshire DE6 1GH
Tel: 01335 343945/346138
Fax: 01335 346488

**British Agrochemicals
Association (BAA)**
4 Lincoln Court, Lincoln Road,
Peterborough PE1 2RP
Tel: 01733 349225 Fax: 01733 62523

**Biotechnology and Biological
Sciences Research Council
(BBSRC)**
Polaris House, North Star Avenue,
Swindon SN2 1UH
Tel: 01793 413200 Fax: 01793 413201

**Confederation of British
Industry (CBI)**
Centre Point, 103 New Oxford Street,
London WC1A 1DU
Tel: 0171 379 7400 Fax: 0171 836 1114
Telex 21331

**Centre for Exploitation of Science
and Technology (CEST)**
5 Berners Road, Islington,
London N1 0PQ
Tel: 0171 354 9942
Fax: 0171 354 4301

**Department of the
Environment (DoE)**
2 Marsham Street,
London SW1P 3EB
Tel: 0171 276 4125/4144

The Environment Agency
Rivers House,, Waterside Drive,
Aztec West,, Almondsbury,
Bristol BS12 4UD
Tel: 01454 62440

**European Crop Protection
Association (ECPA)**
Avenue de Beaulieu - Box 25,
1160, Brussels, Belgium
Tel: +32 2 663 15 50
Fax: +32 2 663 15 60
Telex 62129

**European Initiative for Integrated
Farming (EIF)**
c/o FIP (Fördergemeinschaft
Integrierter Pflanzenbau e V)
Rochusstraße 18A,
53123 Bonn, Germany
Tel: +49 228 97993 30
Fax: +49 228 97993 40

FACTS
c/o BASIS (Registration) Ltd,
2 St John Street, Ashbourne,
Derbyshire DE6 1GH
Tel: 01335 343945/346138
Fax: 01335 346488

Fertiliser Manufacturers Association (FMA)
Greenhill, Thorpe Wood,
Peterborough, PE3 6GF
Tel: 01733 331303
Fax: 01733 333617

Farming and Wildlife Advisory Group (FWAG)
National Agricultural Centre,
Kenilworth, Warwickshire CV8 2RX
Tel: 01203 696699
Fax: 01203 696760

Focus on Farming Practice (FOFP)
CWS Agriculture, The White House,
Stoughton, Leicester LE2 2FL
Tel: 0116 271 4278
Fax: 0116 272 0640

Game Conservancy Trust
Fordingbridge, Hampshire SP6 1EF
Tel: 01425 652381/656713
Fax: 01425 655848

Integrated Arable Crop Production Alliance (IACPA)
c/o Ministry of Agriculture Fisheries and Food (MAFF)
Nobel House, 17 Smith Square,
London SW1P 3JR
Tel: 0171 238 5562
Fax: 0171 238 5597

Linking Environment and Farming (LEAF)
National Agricultural Centre,
Kenilworth, Warwickshire CV8 2LZ
Tel: 01203 413911 Fax: 01203 413636

Less Intensive Farming and the Environment (LIFE)
Institute of Arable Crops Research
(IACR), University of Bristol,
Bristol, Avon BS18 9AF
Tel: 01275 394007

LINK – Integrated Farming Systems (IFS)
High Mowthorpe, Duggleby, Malton,
North Yorkshire YO17 8BP
Tel: 01944 738434

Ministry of Agriculture Fisheries and Food (MAFF)
Nobel House, 17 Smith Square,
London SW1P 3JR
Tel: 0171 238 5562 Fax: 0171 238 5597

National Farmers Union (NFU)
Agriculture House,
164 Shaftesbury Avenue,
London WC2H 8HL
Tel: 0171 331 7200 Fax: 0171 331 7410

Royal Society for the Protection Of Birds (RSPB)
The Lodge, Sandy,
Bedfordshire SG19 2DL
Tel: 01767 680551

Sainsbury's
J Sainsbury plc, Primary Agriculture
Department, Stamford House,
Stamford Street, London SE1 9LL